There Is A Ram In The Bush

UNDERSTANDING THE PROCESS
OF
CHRISTIAN
ALCOHOL AND DRUG RECOVERY

Ronald Simmons

Ronald Simmons

Copyright © 1998 by Ronald Simmons
Los Angeles, California
All rights reserved
Printed and Bound in the United States of America

Published and Distributed by:
Simmons Books
1825 Middleton Place
Los Angeles California 90062
310 764-4400

First Printing, August 1998
10 9 8 7 6 5 4 3 2 1

Second Printing, February 2000

ISBN 1- 881524- 29- 9

All rights reserved. No part of this book may be reproduced in whole or in part, in any form or by any means, electronic or mechanical, including photocopying, recording or by any information storage and retrieval system, without permission in writing from the author. Address inquires to *Simmons Books,* 1825 Middleton Place Los Angeles, California 90062, (310) 764-4400.

<u>Ronald Simmons</u>

Please Note

The word satan is not capitalized: I refused to recognize satan as being important, and capitalizing the name (satan) seems to give him importance.

Table of Contents

Foreword	9
Preface	10
Introduction	13
1. My Journey From Darkness to Light	21
2. Disease of Addiction	27
3. The Addict/alcoholic	34
4. What is the Process of Recovery?	38
5. Why the Process of Recovery?	41
6. There is Power in Being Powerless	43
7. The Recovering Alcoholic/Addict	48
8. Understanding Relapse	51
9. Why a Sponsor	54
10. The Church	58
11. Why so Many Meetings	66
12. Free N One - The Program	69
13. The 12 Spiritual Ways to Recovery	71
14. The 12 Spiritual Ways to Recovery	73
Step 1	73
Step 2	79
Step 3	83
Step 4	88
Step 5	92
Step 6	96
Step 7	98
Step 8	101
Step 9	103
Step 10	105
Step 11	107
Step 12	109

Table of Contents

14. Freedom Towers	112
1st Floor - Throw Up The White Flag	115
2nd Floor - Education	123
3rd Floor - Surrender All	127
4th Floor - Revealing Who We Really Are	135
5th Floor - Exposing Yourself!	140
6th Floor - Look in the Mirror!	144
7th Floor - Eliminate Those Things That Keep us From Growing	146
8th Floor - What Part Did You Have To Play in It?	149
9th Floor - I Apologize	154
10th Floor - Will The Real You Please Stand Up!	156
11th Floor - Work on Yourself!	160
12th Floor - Get to Work	162
15. What Did You Learn From This Process Called Recovery	164
Recovery Card	167

Ronald Simmons

Acknowledgments

Spiritual Leaders

To my Pastor Bishop Charles E. Blake who is a General in God's army, and inspires me to go higher! I thank God for leading me to West Angeles Church of God in Christ.

To sister Blake who is one of the sweetest women of God I have ever met. Thanks for caring.

To Dr. Jeremiah A. Wright, Thank you for opening up doors in the Word of God that I never knew were there.

To Pastor Ronald Wright - To my brother in the Lord. The bible says Iron sharpens Iron. "Thanks Iron." To Pastor Ed "To Tall" Jones - Thanks for your encouragement, it means a lot, and goes very far. To Reverend Frank Wilson - When I was a babe in Christ, and looking for a real Christian Man, God sent me to you. To Bunny Wilson - Powerful sister in the Lord! To Terri McFaddin - Thanks for your teaching, and standing tall in Christ. (You never know who's watching) To Pastor Ron Gibson - great example of someone coming from the hood. I needed to see that.

To Pastor Billy Ingram - My foundation was built at Maranatha, on the Word of God that was preached by you! To Big Daddy - as long as I can remember you have been praying for me, and it was your prayers that prayed me into the family of faith. To Big Mama - can't wait to see you again!

Family & Friends Who put up with me!

To my Mother and Father - thanks for never giving up on me, and teaching me right from wrong. Thanks for teaching me what family is all about, and taking care of me. I Love you so very much!
To Hazel and Annette thanks for loving me! To Don - I miss you so much, can't wait to see you again! To Oscar thanks

Ronald Simmons

Michael & Dora, Little Mike, Candice, Kimberly. Dave, Anthony. Uncle Hank & Aunt Jewell, Rene, Jovan. Tony & John, Jenell, Jena. Terri & Marvin, Adrian, Loren. Eric & Schlanda, Schvonda, Jasmine, Little Eric. To Aunt Ruby, Ryan, Jennifer, Janice. To Henry & Katharine, Freddie, Bobby, Paula, Cleave, Mike, Fredrick. To Willie, Julia, Big Vollon & Marsha, Little Vollon & Grace. Richard & Margaret Easter. Pat & Brandon. Stacy & Alfred (thanks for being good parents) Paula Litt, Sunshine Njeri. To Big Big Less & Lois. Big Less & Wanda & Little Less, Brittany, Brianna. Lamel, Amhrie, Aletrice. Krystal, Tony & Khristina. John & Kim - Jeff & Rochelle - Joe & Diane - Ron & Joyce -Rene and Amin - Carolyn Habersham (you will always be family), Clarence Greenwood and Barbara McFarlin and the Free N One family. Bobby Blue, Furlon Usher. T House & T House Alumni. Alma, Michelle, Richard. The Fellows - Rare Mix Antique Classic Truck Club - Lieutenant & Sheba.

To my wife Yolonda, who prayed for me, stayed by my side and is my best friend. I Love you!

To my son Daniel, I may not say it all the time but I am proud of you. Keep God First.

To my daughter Danyell, I miss you when you're gone! I need someone to debate the issues.

To my daughter Quianna remember you come from a strong black family line. Never stop reaching for the sky!

To my daughter Kamille, yea my daughter thanks for being a good little sister.

Whew! (Sometimes you don't realize how blessed you are until you attempt to count your blessings!

THANK YOU LORD FOR MY FAMILY!

Ronald Simmons

About The Author

Born and raised in Los Angeles, Ron celebrates 17 years of being free from drugs and alcohol. Married to Yolonda Simmons they have three children. Twins Daniel and Danyell 18 years of age, who both attend San Diego State University, 15 year old Quianna who is a sophomore in high school.

Attended El Camino College, and received a certificate in Drug and Alcohol Counseling from UCLA. He has also received awards and commendations from the Mayor of Los Angeles and the Senate.

Ron lectures Nationally on Drug and Alcohol Recovery. Ron co-founded the Nationally ran organization Free N One. Free N One assist Churches in establishing successful outpatient Drug and Alcohol programs at their local Church.

Ron is currently the Executive Director of Transition House, a Christ centered drug and alcohol in-house program owned by the First Jurisdiction of Southern California of the Church of God in Christ, where Bishop Charles E. Blake is the Prelate.

The success of this program is already being highly recognized in the recovery community as an excellent model for Christian recovery homes.

After years of success with Free N One out patient program and the director of Transition House, there has been many request for written help in the form of an instructional manual. Mr. Simmons debuts his first book "THERE IS A RAM IN THE BUSH": Understanding the Process of Christian Drug and Alcohol Recovery.

Ronald Simmons

Foreword

Substance abuse has been recognized by the medical community as a clinically verified disorder. Alcoholism and drug addition have been called "diseases". Much of the discussion concerning treatment for substance abuse has centered around medical, biological, and/or societal factors that influence addition and abusive behavior.

Ron Simmons has written a book that addresses the root of the problem of addition. His approach is to expose drug addition and abuse by going to the core, examining the reason and the patterns for abuse. Self-abuse and abuse of others is first a spiritual matter, with detrimental biological and environmental consequences.

Deliverance from substance abuse is possible and available through faith and obedience to God. This book speaks to the user, the enabler, loved ones of abusers, ministers, educators, and medical professionals. Ron shares useful information that all of us can appreciate.

Ron is qualified to speak on the subject. He is a recovered substance abuser who has assisted in the reclaiming of many lives, for Christ. He is currently the director of Transition House, a facility for recovering substance abusers. The center is owned and operated by the First Jurisdiction of Southern California of the Church of God in Christ. By 1998, more than 20 men completed the program successfully. Ron's commitment to the ministry of counseling and intervention in this area is a testament to the saving power of Jesus Christ. The Transition House provides a Christian based recovery program that works because God's word is true, effective, and life changing!

I hope that you will be inspired by this book. May the inspiration motivate you toward a closer walk with God.

Charles E. Blake, Bishop
First Jurisdiction of Southern California
Member, General Board of the Church of God in Christ

Preface

Should Christian recovery be a better recovery? Should the success rate in Christian out patient programs or in-house facilities be higher than secular ran programs?

As servants of God the result of what we do should be nothing less than excellent. As Christians our job is to reach for perfection, never being in competition with anyone! Our job as Christian facilitators, counselors, therapists, and psychologists is to serve God's people to the best of our ability while serving a perfect God. The Word of God has set high standards for us to follow, always recognizing that even if we fail, there is no failure in God.

So the question should be, can Christian recovery be perfected? Through Gods Word; Yes! As Christian we believe "we can do all things through Christ that strengthen us." As long as we "keep pressing towards the mark of the high calling in Christ Jesus."

Christians have to say yes! Those that work in this field of ministry must say yes, or walk away from this type of ministry.

Recovery is nothing new to God. Recovery is simply explained in the Word of God at Romans 12:2 "and do not be conformed to this world, but be transformed by the renewing of your mind, that you may prove what is that good and acceptable and perfect will of God." Transforming your mind is the key and this does not happen overnight.

Addicts and alcoholics come to the Church understanding, something has to change, but what to change and how to change it, is a mystery. Psychologists today tell us that the disease of addiction centers in our mind, so it would be wise to start our battle with the mind.

One member of Free N One, early in his recovery walked into my office, frustrated with all the changes that were taking place in his life, and cried out "I think you guys are trying to brain wash me!"

First I started to laugh, but then I thought about what he said. Anyone that gets paid on Friday and is broke on Saturday morning, or who drank so much he can't remember how he got home, or what he did the night before, anyone who has a hard time looking at himself in the mirror because of some of the demoralizing things he's done in the pass, this person needs his brain washed!

"The Ram in the Bush" attempts to define the Process of Recovery in such a way that anyone that is called to this ministry will be able to lead any suffering addict/alcoholic on this road to recovery. For the practicing addict/alcoholic that reads this book will understand the work that it takes to be free, and this process does not come over night. The family member will finally see that there is nothing they can do, to keep the addict/alcoholic from using and drinking. They will also realize the work it takes in order for that love one to be free.

The Process of Recovery is a systematic series of actions, which leads the recovering person out of the bondage they are in. Along with the 12 Spiritual Ways, the Process helps in renewing the mind of the addictive persons thinking, and actions. These Steps are designed to take a recovering person by the hand and guide him to better lifestyle, in Christ Jesus. By singling out his character defects and replacing them with moral standards, The recovering person slowly becomes what God wants him to be. In this case the Word of God and the 12 Spiritual Ways assists the addict/alcoholic to lead a better life.

The disease of addiction is cunning, baffling and powerful. Some addicts/alcoholics can't stay free in an outpatient setting, and have to enter into a Christ-centered recovery homes. In these homes, developing a personal relationship with our Lord and Savior Jesus Christ, learning how to get honest with others and with themselves, facing their defects of character, and uncovering years of hidden pain, can be addressed by experienced counselors. In these recovery homes they are also given tools that can help them to live a bondage free lifestyle. I believe God called me to write this book to help educate the Church and Christ-centered recovery homes regarding this Process called Recovery.

INTRODUCTION

Have you ever been bold enough to ask God, "What's really going on"? Or have you ever been straightforward with God and asked Him, "Why are we losing this war on drug and alcohol addiction in the church"?

Or can you even be honest enough with yourself or with God, and say, "yes, we have been losing this war against drug and alcohol addiction," a war that we should be winning, because Jesus is Lord!

All through the Bible God has defeated satan in a mighty way, but here in 1998 we are losing battle after battle. All over the world, every day God's people are getting hooked on some form of drug, or they are trying drugs or trying alcohol for the first time.

Perfectly stable families are being destroyed because the head of that family will try cocaine for the first time, and become a slave to this powerful, illegal drug. Once the head has been chopped off, the rest of the family falls or struggles aimlessly into the night, doing all they can to recover, or survive.

This disease has even come into the House of God! From the usher's board, to the choir stand, to the volunteers, to the pulpit, men and women in the church are falling to this disease we call addiction. In my 14 years of Christian drug and alcohol ministry, I have talked to hundreds of ministers that have personally been effected by this demon. As I talk to some of them, I see and share the pain that they feel when someone close to them--a family member, or someone on their staff, or someone in their congregation--falls to this monster called addiction. Some pastors lose hope and even question their calling, because their many attempts to help addicts or alcoholics have failed. The pain is unbearable, as they watch

God's people return to the hell they once were in. After many failing attempts, some ministers avoid the problem altogether and will send the practicing addict/alcoholic somewhere else, in order not to deal with the pain of another failure. But most hold on tightly and believe God will make a way one day. (We believe that day is today).

Don't get me wrong; the church has won, and is winning many battles daily. Each battle won is still a great miracle, especially to the addict or alcoholic who is delivered, and to his family and loved ones! The day an addict or alcoholic surrenders and turns his or her life over to God, this miracle is equal to that of parting the Red Sea or raising Lazarus from the dead. As a matter of fact the dead have risen, and the people of God rejoice as the addict or alcoholic surrenders and is set free!

We have seen it countless times; a practicing addict or alcoholic will come to the Lord and totally surrender his life to God. The spirit of God moves through this person and this person is delivered with just a touch. But compared to the addicts and alcoholics that are living in the streets, or still at home destroying their lives, and their families' lives, we are losing the war.

For those of us who believe in Jesus with all our hearts and souls, and have been part of this Free N One ministry, we know this is a winnable war, and we center our hope in the fact that Jesus is Lord and we serve a victorious God!

We know this is a winnable war, we see the captured being set free daily. In the days of our bondage, most of us walked through the doors of many churches looking for help! Hoping that this revival would work, or this healing service would work, only to return to the walking dungeon of death we were in. But God has a "Ram in the bush!"

So the question has to be asked! What is the church doing wrong? We, the children of God, who have been called to be a light for those who are still in darkness! What are we doing wrong? We who have seen God move mountains in our own lives, and work miracles in countless others! We who know that there is no failure in God! What are we doing wrong? Or more important the question should be "what can we do right to help our people who are slowly dying from satan's attacks?"

In this book "There is a Ram in the Bush," we first understand our enemy, and how he attacks! Most people will be surprised to see that the enemy attacks long before the first drink or the first hit! But satan's job is to magnify the drugs and alcohol. Even though we gather our armies and build up our warriors, they are non-effective if we send them in the wrong direction. Today, because of the process of recovery, the church now comes together as one to attack the enemy!

Next you have to put the right people in the right place! Not everyone will be able to lead the charge into battle! For instance, not everybody can work in the children's church, and not everybody can sing in the choir, so surely not everybody can work in the drug and alcohol ministry. Even though they may have a burden for God's people in this area, not everyone can do the work.

Have you ever listened to a bad choir sing? We praise God for their effort and give them credit for making a joyful noise unto the Lord, but some of the notes they are singing have not been invented yet. The same thing happens in the ministry of drug/alcohol addiction. If you have the wrong person in charge of this ministry, or the wrong people leading the battle, this ministry will never be effective. Unlike hearing a few bad notes from a not-so-polished choir, we have lost a soul who could be free from this bondage, if the right people were in place. We believe this ministry should be led by people that God has delivered from this bondage. I would not want the first lady of my church walking into some of the dope houses, gambling shacks, and gang-infested areas that I use to feel comfortable in. (Even though I know she would because she is filled with God's spirit.)

Today I know God kept me safe, and allowed me to go through everything that I went through, that I might go back to that type of hell and guide others out!

Once you get your army together, you have to train this army with which weapons to use, and how to use them, and when to use them. The Bible says, "my people perish because of a lack of knowledge. I have personally witnessed many Christ-centered drug and alcohol programs that looked great on paper, but were non-effective because they were using the wrong weapons for this particular battle!

Finally we need to know what medicine should be used to completely heal the wounded and who will be coming for help. One of the most frustrating things for anyone, who works in this field, is to watch a person relapse. (Go back out and use or drink.) There is no pain like watching a loved one, who God brings out of that type of hell, seeing him get his family, his job, and the respect of his peers back. We are also there with him to celebrate, 6 months, 9 months, 1 year, clean and sober, giving God all the Glory! And then one day he turns around, and we watch him return to the hell he once was in. It is like pulling the plug in a sink filled with water. It drains the hope out of the addict and most people involved. The wounded need to know just what "spiritual" medicine to take, to keep them free "one day at a time" forever!

I believe this book addresses these issues and many more. It is also an attempt to bring the church together as one. One united front standing together, and we will start seeing more victories in larger battles. I believe this war is a winnable war because we serve a victorious God!

In 1981 I was introduced to this process called recovery. It took me a whole year to get serious about working and living my program. For the first year I was excited about being free from the pains of every-day using. Participating in 12-step meetings, I had learned enough to know that just being free from drugs and alcohol was not enough.

Ronald Simmons

It was at this time I accepted Christ into my life, and my whole life turned around. As far as this new life was concerned, I was a babe in Christ, and I was a babe at living. I didn't know how to pay bills, wash my own clothes, or cook for myself. I didn't know how to deal with my anger, or recognize my feelings. On the other hand Church was foreign to me. I didn't know the difference between a deacon and a minister, or a Pastor and a Reverend. I did not have a clue what a Bishop's job was! Bottom line, I did not know how to live, I knew nothing about living life on life's terms, and how to be a real man, I didn't have a clue.

Once I started working this process, it was suggested that I get a sponsor. A sponsor is a person who has been through the process of recovery. (See chapter on sponsor) He has applied all 12 steps in his life, and is willing to help me walk through these same 12 steps. Then I met a brother in the Church who took me under his wings, and walked with me according to the Word of God. I loved this new life!

In recovery, I found that I had a special love for all recovering people who were, after all, just like me. I understood those who were struggling to stay free from this disease, one day at a time. We went to 12-step meetings and sober functions together. They became my new friends.

In the Church I enjoyed praising God together with the Saints. I also enjoyed going to Bible studies with other believers and learning how to be a Christian. As I grew in the Lord, I knew it was only God that kept me free from my addictions.

During this time it was OK for me to be a babe in Christ, and a babe in recovery. I could ask all kinds of questions about recovery and about life. It was explained to me that the only dumb question was an unasked question!

As my relationship with God grew, one question began to pull at my soul. Why were there so many addicts suffering from this disease? I personally witnessed what God was doing in the anonymous programs, even if the anonymous programs didn't give God all the glory. They said things like "Get a God of your understanding" or "if that light is your God let it be your God"! This bothered me a great deal, but I witnessed people being freed from their addictions.

In the church, I witnessed the power of God in the "laying on of hands". With one touch from God, I have seen people healed from this disease. On the other hand, those addicts and alcoholics that were being freed in the Church were small compared to those being healed in the anonymous programs. This bothered me because I knew that we served a mighty and powerful God. A God that was first in everything, first in healing, first in recovery, and first in living. I knew my God could do anything.

Deep down in my soul I knew God had put the anonymous programs together, but somewhere down the line they had gotten away from praising God and giving God all the Glory! Growing in the Word of God and at the same time applying the 12 steps of recovery into my life, I found scriptures that supported the 12 steps! God revealed to me that He wanted me to bring recovery to the church, and bring Jesus to the anonymous programs!

Before I started this ministry, there was one question that had to be answered.

Why is it that some addicts can have hands laid on them and be delivered from drugs and alcohol addiction, and others can not?

These are some of the answers that I received from the church:

A. The person laying on of hands is not anointed.
B. The person laying on of hands does not have enough faith.
C. The person receiving (the addict/alcoholic) really does not want to receive his healing.

D. The person receiving does not know how to receive his healing.
E. The person receiving has a lack of faith.

When I would hear those answers from C - E, they would bring tears to my eyes. For some reason, some people actually believed that the addict was doing something wrong. I remember every time they laid hands on me, I really wanted to quit. Today when I hear this it still bothers me. I wonder how many addicts have heard this, and walked away feeling God didn't love them!

So when freedom does not happen for addicts/alcoholics they walk away believing:

1. God doesn't love them.
2. This is all fake.
3. The Church is a rip off.
4. Maybe there is something wrong with me.

The Bible says, "My people perish because of a lack of knowledge." As I attempt to answer this question, you will see, the lack of knowledge comes from both parties- Church and the addictive person.

As I continue to study the Word, and to apply God's principles in my life. I realize that I have been called to God's ministry in two areas.

To work with addicts/alcoholics, teaching them how to be free, and to understand the disease of addiction.

To teach the Church the Process of Recovery, and show them how to walk with that person who is in recovery!

Today, after 14 years in the ministry I believe I have an answer to the question, "Why is it that some addicts can have hands laid on them and be delivered from drugs and alcohol addiction, and others can't?"

Ronald Simmons

Here we go!

1. Let's look at those who came to the altar and allowed the Man of God to lay hands on them, and never used drugs and alcohol again. This group of now delivered addicts/alcoholics left the altar with made-up minds, surrendering everything! On that day they gave up the old friends, the old playgrounds, cigarettes, alcohol, drugs, the whole life style!

2. On the other hand, there were those who came to that same altar, to that same Man of God on that same day, left the church and continued participating in their addiction. (I'm in this group.) So what was the difference? This group came to the altar to be delivered from drugs and alcohol only! Not to be delivered from the life style. After spending time with the addicts/alcoholics who continued to practice their disease, we found that they all had these things in common: 1. Disobedience 2. Selfishness 3. Pride and 4. Denial.

These four character defects God hates, and they must be dealt with before true freedom can take place. Remember these same four defects got satan kicked out of heaven!

We thank God for plan A, the laying on of hands, but we also thank God for plan B, or God's "ram in the bush" called recovery! God, in His Word gives this process of recovery to us. Because of a lack of knowledge, or because we were always looking for plan A, (laying on of hands) we missed plan B, the process of recovery. To the Church there is a "RAM IN THE BUSH." And that ram in the bush is "THE PROCESS OF RECOVERY."

We thank God for plan "B" (Recovery). We know that plan A, the laying on of hands, is real and powerful. But for some strange reason everyone does not receive this power. So they leave the Church frustrated, with no hope.

I believe one of my callings while I am here on this earth is to educate the Church on the process of recovery!

Ronald Simmons

Chapter One

MY JOURNEY FROM DARKNESS TO LIGHT

Born and raised on the East Side of Los Angeles, California. Ron grew up in a loving home with two sisters and one brother. After witnessing the Watts riots, Ron knew that Los Angeles was a dangerous place to live, but he felt well protected by his mother and father, who worked hard to give their family every thing they needed.

When Ron was ten, his family moved to Inglewood, California. At this time, Inglewood was predominately white, and was considered a very safe place to live. Yet it was in Inglewood that Ron and his brother had their first encounter with racism. It was also in Inglewood that Ron found out he was a Black human being in a racist society.

During Ron's middle school years, most of the whites began to move out of the neighborhood, and African Americans began moving in. Slowly, Inglewood was being split in half. The East side of Inglewood was 70% black, and the West side was 98% White.

In 1969, a year before Ron was to enroll into Morningside High School, a law was passed that would change his life forever. The children in his neighborhood were bussed to Inglewood high school. Inglewood was located on the West Side, and was an all white high school.

That very first day was a day Ron and his friends would never forget. There were two hundred African American kids pulling up in big yellow busses to a school that had two thousand whites. White people were picketing with signs that read, "nigger, go home," parents were arguing, and the kids got off the bus, fighting. The police were called in, and people on both sides went to jail. Ron recalled that, on that day, one white person argued so much that he had a heart attract, and had to be rushed to the hospital.

In the coming month there were many debates, many fights, and many suspensions, Eventually, the physical fighting died down, but the moral fights continued on.

While this was going on at Inglewood High, there were fights brewing deep on the east and south sides of Los Angeles. Black gangs were being formed and black on black crime was growing fast. The blacks at Inglewood received news of these gangs, and found it hard to believe, especially when they were fighting racism in Inglewood!

It was 1972, when the notorious gang called the "crips," crossed the line at Inglewood High and stabbed one of Ron's best friends.

Ron recalls the events after the stabbing. "I will never forget seeing little Tex' lying up in the hospital, with tubes going all through his body. It was on that day that my friends and I pledged our allegiance to the newly formed 'family gang'. (Now called the 'blood gang').

"From 1972 to 1974, I was in gang fights, shoot outs, and today I know it was God that kept me from being killed!"

"In the family gang, I was given numerous street names, shot gun slim, Old English, and Brougham. They gave me the name "shot gun slim' because I carried a saw-off, and I was a very skinny kid. "Old English" because I drank Old English 800 malt liquor all the time, and Brougham in my later days, because like the Cadillac I considered my self to be the top of the line.

"To this day I credit my mother and father for making me keep my grades up. No matter how crazy I became, you could not bring a "D" of an "F" into my parent's home. I believe I was the only gang member that had to keep his grades up!

"In my last years of high school, I began to experiment with marijuana, and hard liquor. Chasing women started to overrule gang banging.

"Because of my encounter with racism, I hated gang banging with all my heart. It was not something I wanted to do! It was something that I felt I had to do. Those early years at Inglewood high school gave me an education like no other. The bond between the African American kids at that school was stronger than most family structures. Nobody liked us, not the whites on the inside of the school, nor the "crips" on the outside of the school. We stuck together like glue, because it was too dangerous to be caught alone.

"In 1974, my last year of high school, my closest friends and I made a decision to quit banging. Everyone had his or her reasons for quitting, but mine was easy. The women that I wanted to date didn't like gang members.

"In my last year at Inglewood high, my mother and father divorced, and in my attempt to help out the household I chose selling marijuana. In the beginning, I saw it as taking care of myself and not being a burden on my mother. But as the money got longer and bigger, I fell in love with the life style. The more money I had the more power I had, and unbeknownst to be these two combinations brought women, which turned out to be right up my alley.

"After graduating from Inglewood, I enrolled into El Camino College. While I was there I continued to sell marijuana, only now on a large scale, until one day I felt school was getting in the way of my business. I quit school and sold dope full time.

"By the age of 20 I was selling drugs all over the country, and decided that I would sell drugs for the rest of my life. By this time I had been introduced to all types of drugs, PCP, heroin, and cocaine, but cocaine turned out to be my main source of income. At 24, I started manufacturing crack cocaine and selling it in large quantities. At 25 my habit had grown to $800.00 a day, surely, I had become my best customer.

"In April of 1981, with the help of my family, I admitted myself into a drug rehabilitation program. In that rehab, a nurse re-introduced me to God and told me about Jesus. Every night before she left work, she would come into my room and share a scripture with me and tell me to read something in the Bible.

"After leaving that rehab, I joined a gym at one of the local parks in Inglewood and became a dedicated body builder. It was here at this gym I met some brothers that loved the Lord, and they shared the word with me every day. It was in that gym that I accepted Jesus Christ as my personal Lord and Savior.

"I continued my after-care program by getting involved with Narcotics Anonymous (NA), and Alcoholics Anonymous (AA). Cocaine Anonymous (CA) had not been formed, but today I attend those meeting as well. In these programs, I made a lot of new friends, and learned a lot about myself.

"I also stayed in contact with the nurse that shared the Word of God with me for the first time. She became my prayer partner, and I joined the church, which she attended. For four years, I sat under that ministry which was, and still is a Word-driven Church. It was Maranatha Community Church; pastored by Billy Ingram, that God spoke to me about a Christ centered 12 -step program for the Church.

I presented this vision to Pastor Ingram and he allowed me to start a Christ centered meeting called "habit free". Addicts and alcoholics flocked to this meeting and for the first time in my life it felt like I was doing something right.

There was one thing wrong with this meeting. Addicts and alcoholics would come to the meeting on a Wednesday night, and by Saturday many of them were getting high, or drinking. Once again God spoke to me, and told me to copy a program that He already had in place, Alcoholic Anonymous. God shared with me one of the reasons Alcoholic Anonymous, Narcotic Anonymous, and Cocaine Anonymous were so successful. They had meetings for the recovering person every night of the week. It was then that I contacted Ronald Wright, now the Rev. Ron Wright, and pastor of his own Church. I heard Ron share at a NA meeting, and in his pitch he talked about how God had saved his life. Ron also belonged to a Church that was not afraid of being on the front line. I also witnessed another brother, named Rene Whitehead, sharing about the power of God, and how God brought him out of his addiction. He was also attending a front line Church.

I called these brothers together in the summer of 1988, and we formed the now nationally known organization Free N One drug and alcohol program. Now there are meetings all over the nation. Pastors and church leaders are calling from all over the country, wanting more information about Free N One. Not long after starting God's Free N One program, we noticed that we were missing a very important part of the ministry, the family members. God allowed us to see that the addict or the alcoholic was now being freed from his bondage, but the family member who had stood by him had also been tremendously affected by his usage. It was then that we started a support meeting called Free N One's "Tough Love". In these meetings, the family members who have been broken can slowly learn how to let God put his/her lives back together through God's Word.

Ronald Simmons

In 1989 God led me to move my Church membership to West Angeles Church of God in Christ, Bishop Charles E. Blake is the Pastor. I was brought on staff as head of the substance abuse department. Every Friday night, our substance abuse committee holds a Free N One meeting at West Angeles. We also have a Saturday women only Free N One meeting. We also hold a Free N One Tough Love meeting, and we meet in one-on-one setting with people that have been effected by drugs and alcohol.

In 1991, Bishop Charles E. Blake asked me to head the 1st Jurisdiction of Southern California COGIC (Church of God in Christ) Transition House. This house is a 10-bed facility for men that need more than meetings and have to remove themselves from their current environment in order to get well. The success of Transition House has been nothing short of a miracle! Men are finding freedom and turning their lives over to Jesus.

Ron returned to UCLA, and received his certificate in drug and alcohol counseling and alcohol and drug studies. He has received many awards and commendations from the mayor of Los Angeles and from the Senate.

On April 22, 1998 Ron will celebrate 17 years of being drug and alcohol free.

He is married to Yolonda Simmons, and they have three children. The twins Daniel & Danyell, are 18 years of age, and attend San Diego State University. Fifteen year old Quiana is in her second year of high school. They are very proud of their father's recovery and ministry.

Chapter Two

THE DISEASE OF ADDICTION
Disease – illness, infirmity, affliction, sickness.

By the time most addicts or alcoholics realize they have problems, they are mentally exhausted, physically destroyed, and spiritually bankrupt. This is caused by countless attempts to stop, and then always returning, sometimes drinking and using more than before.

Alcoholism and drug addiction is considered a disease by most major medical associations in the world today. This illness is characterized by continued drinking or continued substance abuse. It is very important that the recovering person recognize that he or /she has a disease.

Once a recovering person understands, and accepts the fact that he is sick, he can start seeking treatment for his illness. Like any other disease, if left untreated, the disease of alcoholism or addiction will only worsen. One reason most addicts/ alcoholics struggle so long is because they believe they can return to sociable drinking and using. They don't realize that once you cross that "fine invisible line" into addiction or alcoholism, there is no turning back, and the disease gets progressively worse every time you take a drink or a hit. The disease causes a craving beyond mental control, and no matter what defense you try, you return to abusing drinking and using. Some will try changing their choice of drug or alcohol. They believe that by changing to a so-called lesser substance, the problem will be fixed. The cocaine or heroin addict will change to marijuana, and the scotch or hard drinker will change to drinking beer or wine; only to find out that this does not fix them or work for them, and they end up returning to the drug or alcohol of their choice--once again using and abusing!

Some addicts or alcoholics make desperate attempts to stop using by blaming the people in their immediate circle or area in which they live. So they move from neighborhood to neighborhood, city to city, or state to state running from what they think is the problem. Only to find out that they cannot run from themselves. We in recovery call this "doing a geographic." One writer wrote "everywhere you go, there you are."

Once a recovering person understands he is ill, he can begin taking the right prescription or medicine, that will relieve him of the pain and aggravation he is experiencing. When ministering to recovering addicts/alcoholics, one of the first things we try to do is express that they are not bad people trying to be good, but they are sick people trying to get well!

Even though addiction is a disease, most people regard it differently from any other disease. There is pity for a person that has cancer or HIV, but for an addict or alcoholic there is anger, resentment and frustration. Some think because they brought it upon themselves, they should live with the choices they made. Others believe that they should just stop and this problem will go away. Unfortunately, it's not that easy. This sickness has to be confronted and dealt with before freedom will come.

For every sickness there is a cause! In recovery we look for the cause and center our medication towards that cause. The causes of high blood pressure are the foods we eat, the stress of life, and lack of exercise. Addiction is a spiritual disease that centers in our mind, caused by disobedience to God's Word, and a need to satisfy the flesh. This is why the Bible says we must "renew the mind." (Ephesians 4:23)

Because of God's Word we know there are character flaws in every human being. (No man is perfect, no, not one) For the addict or alcoholic, there are two flaws that stand out, and must be addressed. These are "pride and selfishness." Our selfishness usually gets us started! "It's my thing, I do what I want to do" attitude. Pride tells us, "It cannot happen to me," These two character defects are very noticeable in every alcoholic or addict that we have encountered. As the disease gets progressively worse, pride and selfishness rises higher and higher. We have found that it is even harder for the Christian addict or alcoholic in this area! We hear things like "I'm saved, sanctify, filled with the Holy Ghost, I don't need no meetings!" So they lean unto their own understanding and most of the time these are the first to get loaded, or take a drink!

The Bible tells a story about a man that loved the Lord with all his heart, but because of his pride he was afflicted by an illness! (II Corinthian 12:7-10) -- "To keep me from becoming conceited because of these surpassingly great revelations, there was given me a thorn in my flesh, the messenger of Satan, to torment me. (v8) Three times I pleaded with the Lord to take it away from me." (v9) But he said to me, 'My Grace is sufficient for thee, for my strength is made perfect in weakness. Therefore I will boast all the more gladly about my weaknesses, so "that the power of Christ power may rest up on me." (v10) That is why, for Christ's sake, I delight in weaknesses, in insults, in hardships, in persecutions, in difficulties. "For when I am weak I am strong."

Here in this passage we see that because of Paul's conceit (being out of God's will) a thorn was given to him. We know this thorn was not a "rose bush thorn" piercing his flesh. Some historians believe this thorn was an illness. Since we do not know what type of illness it was, for the sake of argument, let us say it was some form of addiction. Paul asks three times for the thorn to be taken out of his flesh. God said, "my Grace is sufficient for you."

Let's take a look at this picture. Here's Paul, a true man of God, and a man who wrote 13 books of the Bible suffering from an illness. He asks God to relieve him of this affliction, not once but three (3) times. After each request, God does not honor his prayer! He only says "my grace is sufficient for you". So many times Christians ask God to relieve them of this disease of addiction. Because we have been fighting against the drugs or alcohol, and not what caused us to take drugs and alcohol, we keep spinning our wheels.

The disease of addiction and alcoholism lies dormant inside the recovering person, like a monster that has been locked down and arrested. Just like the thorn stayed with Paul! The Bible never says that God took the thorn from Paul. It is the grace of God that keeps a person free. It has been documented that for addicts and alcoholics that return to drinking and using after years of freedom, it feels as if they had never stopped drinking or using. The pain, the agony, the fear, the guilt, they all returns as if they had never left. When a person returns to using, he/she frees that monster that had been locked down to continue destroying the now practicing addict/alcoholic. The Bible says, in II Peter 2:22, it's like a dog returning to his own vomit.

When God said, "my grace is sufficient for you," He was saying I am not taking this affliction from you, but it is my power that is keeping you from the pain and suffering that it can cause. It is My grace that is giving you peace, and in order to stay free from the pain, you must surrender all to Me.

So in II Corinthian 12: 9-10, like Paul, I will boast all the more gladly about my weakness [the thorn or disease is still with him] so "that Christ's power may rest on me." (v.10) That is why "for Christ's sake," I delight in weaknesses, in insults, in hardships, persecutions, in difficulties, "for when I am weak I am strong."

Here, because of the thorn in his flesh, Paul boasts about his affliction. At verse (10), Paul delights in everything that is supposed to keep him down, or destroy him. For when he is weak, then and only then, does he become strong.

So today it's OK to say that you are a "recovering, delivered, redeemed, blessed, happy alcoholic/addict!"

Some people in the Church will never understand this concept. Unfortunately, it takes a near death experience, or a bondage such as alcoholism, or drug addiction, to understand what God is saying. When I humble myself, I recognize I have no power to fight this bondage. God has all power!

So the question need to be asked, what makes a person return to that hell, that addiction? Remember it was Paul's conceit that brought on the thorn in his flesh. (v.7)

Here are just a few reasons people become re-addicted:

The recovering person steps out of God's will by allowing pride and ego to rise in his/her life. This, in turn, leads to lying, cheating, sexual misconduct, and disobedience to God. Once we get out of God's will, the thorn is released, and the pain and suffering that caused this addiction returns, stronger than ever.

The recovering person arrives, or becomes well, thinking he/she is cured from this disease. So they stop working on themselves. Releasing the monster inside, they never look at the cause and continue to concentrate on the drugs or alcohol.

Psychologists have found that 5% of a recovering person's problem is drugs and alcohol, and 95%--the person himself. Pride, arrogance, selfishness, sexual misconduct, all causes a recovering addict to return to what he knows best, and that is getting high! When you get out of God's will, the only other will is Satan's. There is no in-between. Once you start participating in these old behaviors, the sleeping giant (Addiction/Alcoholism) is awakened, and the only thing that can arrest that monster again is the Power of God through repentance.

Unfortunately some addicts/alcoholics have to hit another bottom before they surrender again. Never forget every bottom has a trap door! The most cunning, powerful, yet baffling, component of this disease is its ability to convince a recovering person that he/she is OK!

Satan deceives hundreds and hundreds of recovering alcoholic/addicts into believing that they are well or normal. So they will go out and take one drink or one hit or one fix. Forgetting the disease factor, and that one drink, hit, or fix turns into two, three and so on. Like an out-of-control train racing downhill, they cannot stop, and they find themselves once again on the bottom, using and abusing.

The disease of addiction is cunning; it will deceive a person, and tell him he is doing OK, and this person will stop working on himself. The disease is also baffling. It will confuse, bewilder, and frustrate the user and slowly steal the self-esteem and joy from his life. The disease is also powerful; it will consume, control and destroy everything and everyone that gets in its path.

The Bible says in II Peter 5: 8, " the devil is like a roaring lion seeking whom he may devour." Never underestimate the disease of addiction. Satan's job is to kill, steal, and destroy! Many Christians have been deceived into thinking that they can go back to sociable drinking and using. The disease of addiction is real and can be arrested only if the addict/alcoholic takes the right medicine.

For the Christian counselor entering into this field of addiction, he must be ready to see the disobedience in every addict/alcoholic that asks for help. It is our disobedience that has allowed Satan to have his way with our lives. And as long as we allow a little sin in, we will be subjected to anything that satan has to offer.

The roaring lion is looking for disobedient Christians, and once they are found, that lion will destroy them by any means necessary. We have to teach our people how to be "on guard," watching and praying, and also honestly examining ourselves daily, to see if we are being doers of the Word in all our affairs.

Ronald Simmons

Chapter Three

THE ADDICT/ALCOHOLIC

Addict -- (1) a slave to a practice. (2) To devote or surrender oneself to something, habitually or obsessively. (3) one who is dependent on drugs or alcohol.

To be a slave to a practice means no matter how hard we try, we continue to drink and use, even when we don't want to.

To devote or surrender oneself to something habitually or obsessively means once the disease of addiction sets in, we spend most of our waking moments using or drinking or thinking about how we are going to use or drink. And once we start we never stop at "just one." We use or drink until there is no more. (One hit is too many and a thousand never enough.)

And finally, one who depends on drugs: An addict or alcoholic will do things that they never believed in a hundred years they would do! They will steal, lie, cheat, sell their bodies, and hurt the people that they love; not because they want to, but because they have to!

There is no set description of an addict. An addict can be black, white, big, small, rich or poor. Addicts have great jobs, addicts are unemployed; they come from good and loving families, and they come from broken homes. An addict can be a Christian, or an addict can be a non-believer. There is one thing that all addicts have in common; no one wants to be one! No one takes their first drink, or smokes their first joint, or takes their first hit of cocaine, and says to themselves, "I am going to be a slave to this forever, and someday this is going to destroy me!"

In the beginning, Satan deceives the person into thinking that he or she is having fun. Music will sound better, communicating with other people, especially the opposite sex, will be easier. Soon problems will arise, but instead of facing those problems we run to drugs and alcohol for escape. We must remember Satan's job is to tell us a lie. Soon the fun is gone, or as one songwriter wrote, "the thrill is gone." But we continue to use drugs. Now we need that drink or that fix! It seems as if we can not function without it.

In the beginning some of us fall to peer pressure. We start drinking and using in order to be accepted by our friends. "To be in the in-crowd." Eat, drink, and be merry, this is all we seek out of life. Satan has shown us another lie and we fall for it. Either way, once you get started, you enter into a world that is controlled by Satan. This is why it is best to never get started. For those of us who did get started, we have crossed that "invisible line" into addiction and alcoholism, and we will do anything for a hit or a drink. Stealing, lying, cheating, even breaking the law to support our habit, is nothing for an addict.

We use the phrase "invisible line" because no one knows the day on which you become addicted. No one knows how much you have to smoke or drink! It just happens.

Some people drink and use and never become addicted. They are able to "drink sociably," they have no problem taking a sip of wine and putting it down. This is not so for the alcoholic, they have to drink until it is all gone.

Some therapists believe the only thing that can stop this person from using is what in recovery we call "hitting a bottom," or "coming to the end of your rope." A bottom can be anything from family and loved ones leaving, to losing their jobs, or losing homes. A bottom can be going to jail or having a near death experience, or losing everything you own. A bottom can happen in any city ghetto, or in the privacy of your expensive home! For the addict/alcoholic a bottom is degrading, demoralizing, and embarrassing. If there is one good thing about hitting a bottom, once you are on the bottom all you can do is look up. (Look up to Jesus!) When an addict hits a bottom, there is no more fight left. There is no more denial, and the addict has to agree that his drinking and using is a huge problem.

Waiting for this addict/alcoholic to hit a bottom can be very trying on family members and friends! It is not easy to watch a loved one destroy himself! The disease of addiction is so cunning, and baffling, some addict's or alcoholics are the last ones to know that they have a problem. Even though he or she has lost weight, can't keep a steady job, is in and out of jail, slowly destroying themselves and the loved ones around them, they never see what the disease of addiction is doing to them. (Or they refuse to take a good look.)

There are some things that loved ones can do to raise the bottom to meet the addicted person. (But this takes courage!) It will take everyone who is close to the addict or alcoholic. The bottom can be raised faster than waiting for the addict/alcoholic to actually hit bottom! Once again this takes courage, faith in God, and participation from all parties involved. Here are two ways: (1) Family and friends must agree not to support the addict financially. Continue to pray for him, and always suggest recovery homes, that you personally will do your best to get them into. (2) Today's therapist uses a strategy called intervention. When the family member chooses "Intervention" five things take place.

A trained therapist is called in to conduct the intervention. The therapist will gather as many family members, loved ones, co-workers, and employers together as possible without the addicted person's knowledge.

Then the therapist will meet with these people who will be involved in the intervention, letting them know that this will be done out of love and not out of anger! It is the therapist's job to make sure the intervention does not turn into a lynch mob, every one present should love and care about the addict/alcoholic.

Next the addict/alcoholic is brought to this meeting place, where each person shares how much he or she cares about him, and how much she loves him. They share about the good times before drugs/alcohol, and the changes that they have witnessed since he began to using drugs or alcohol. The therapist at this time is a silent partner, making sure things do not get out of hand, and there is no cross talk. The therapists also make sure no one is there to mentally beat up the addict or alcoholic, and every thing is done decently and in order.

After every one has shared, from kids to co-workers, the addict or alcoholic is given a chance to share, and the therapist will end this session by offering a drug/alcohol treatment program to the alcoholic/addict.

Unfortunately, intervention may not work for every addicted person. At this point he has the option to continue doing what he has been doing, and the family members have to band together and allow this person to hit a bottom.

We have seen some cases where the addicted person will leave the intervention and find help on their own. Unfortunately if they continue to practice drinking and using, jails, institutions, and death are the only things left. All we can do is continue to pray, and ask God to give us peace in this situation.

Once the practicing addict/alcoholic gets help, he or she moves into recovery and the process begins. This person is now referred to as a Recovering alcoholic/addict.

Chapter Four

WHAT IS THE PROCESS OF RECOVERY?

Definition of Process: (1) a systematic series of actions directed to some end; (2) a continuous action, operation, or series of changes taking place in a definite manner:

Definition of Recovery: (1) regaining something that is lost or taken away. (2) Regaining strength, composure, balance of one self. (3) Restoration or return to any former and better condition, esp. to health from sickness, injury, addiction, etc.

The Process of Recovery was designed for addicts and alcoholics who have hit a spiritual, mental, and physical bottom. The process of recovery is not limited to just addicts and alcoholics. We have found that any one who has lost his composure, or has fallen and cannot get up, as far as living is concerned, can use, or be a part of, this process!

The process of recovery is described as "the last house on the block" for many addicts/alcoholics. Most of us have tried everything conceivable to quit drinking and using. Some run to Church thinking that this will fix them. But without a serious relationship with God, many run back and forth, in and out, of the Church, never experiencing true freedom.

Some try psychiatry, hypnosis, medically prescribed drugs, and even acupuncture to rid themselves of their addiction. For some this may work, but the majority seem to return to the bondage they were in.

Addicts and alcoholics have been known to make geographical moves, going from state to state, city to city, neighborhood to neighborhood, always finding themselves in another city or state doing the same thing. One writer wrote, "everywhere you go there you are."

Some have even gone so far as to be incarcerated purposely, hoping this problem will disappear. This doesn't work because the disease centers in your mind, and as long as you can remember, the disease will be with you. Second, this type of logic will never work because the disease has not been dealt with. The third reason why this will not work, there are a lot of drugs in jail.

The final act of separation from this disease is suicide. The pain becomes so great some people would rather die than live the way they have been living.

In this process God meets you wherever you are, and guides you back to a safe place in Him. Step by step, precept by precept, the process will teach you how to live a successful life in Him. Simple things that we take for granted will be offered to you in this process. These simple principles will bring order back into your life.

The twelve spiritual steps to recovery are purposely arranged in the order that they are for a reason. The first three-(3) steps of recovery introduce you to God. Without God we lean to our own understanding. We must never forget that we were doing our best thinking and we still became addicts or alcoholics. So put no trust in your own logic. Again, renew the mind.

In recovery we share with others who are just like us-- recovering people who are doing all they can to change and apply this process in their lives, sharing how they made it through difficult situations without drinking or using. The big book of Alcoholics Anonymous says one alcoholic helping another is therapeutic. Remember God works through people, so don't be afraid to share your feelings, decisions, your ups and downs, and victories with other people.

The next four (4) steps introduce you to you! From the time you took your very first drink, you altered your course in life, and the path that God had set for you. The more you drank and used, the further away you became! Once you became an addict/alcoholic you also became a fake, phony and fraud. Most addicts/alcoholics have a very small glimpse of "who" they really are. (And others are not sure about that).

These next two (2) steps help you to understand your relationship with people who are close to you. Your loved ones, your family members, your close friends have all been affected by your behavior. Many bridges have been destroyed because of your drinking and using, and at these two steps we get honest about our actions. They have a saying in the program, "What part did you have to play in it?" God is able to fix any bridge that has been destroyed, if you trust in Him and apply this process in your life and allow it to work for you.

The last three (3) steps are called maintenance steps. As you live your life one day at a time, these steps help you keep focused on your recovery and on your growth in God.

Here at the process no one can do the work for you! You have to do it for yourself. Be not afraid, God will never leave you or forsake you! The process of recovery works, but it takes work on your part.

Chapter Five

WHY THE PROCESS OF RECOVERY?

Why the process of recovery? We believe that this is God's ram in the bush! We have seen God work miracles in the lives of practicing alcoholics/addicts! With one touch, healing can take place. With one touch, the power of the Holy Spirit has set some people free faster than you can blink an eye! Still the question arises, and has to be confronted. What about the addict or alcoholic who walks into that same church, on that same day, and gets hands laid on them by the same man of God, and yet return to drinking and using? What is wrong with them? Or does the Church have an answer that will rescue them?

Yes, God has an answer for them! Yes there is a ram in the bush! We believe this ram in the bush is called the "process of recovery!" We who have been freed through this process thank God for this "ram in the bush."

The process of recovery will help anyone who wants help. The process will meet you right where you are. If you are homeless, or have spent most of your life in and out of jail, the process will meet you, and change you if you are willing. If you are a functional addictive person, meaning, you still have a job, and your family members still love you, and they have not broken all ties with you, yet! The process will meet you where you are. You do not have to hit a destructive bottom to get help!

The process helps you to get honest with yourself, and in turn shows you who you really are. It also teaches you how to surrender to God daily. It always reminds you that you are not in control of your life. The process teaches you that there is a power greater than your self! Then it will introduce you to "the" power, Christ Jesus our Lord and Savior, who has all power!

Once you have developed a personal relationship with God, He will show you, with the help of a counselor or sponsor, some of those bad habits that you picked up while you were separated from Him. Once you learn how to recognize these defects of character, the process teaches you how to walk through some of these situations in a different manner, and thus you grow! Each step through the Process will open up doors that we avoided while we were in our addiction. The process of recovery will help us to identify and face our feelings, good or bad, when we go through the pains of life without getting loaded.

Chapter Six

THERE IS POWER IN BEING POWERLESS

If there was ever a concept in the Bible, or in the field of recovery, that logically makes no sense at all, this is it. Receiving power after willingly becoming powerless!
   (1Peter 5:6 Humble yourselves under the mighty hand of God, that he may exalt you in due time.) Humbling yourself, denying yourself, receiving no glories, claming no power of your own, and in return God investing you with all power! Like I said it makes no sense.
   Here we must accept Jesus Christ as our personal Lord and Savior to understand this concept. You must have a "spiritual third eye" to "see" this powerful insight.
   The world, the unsaved, will have a hard time understanding this Godly law. To the World 2+ 2 has to equal 4. Willingly becoming powerless, and God giving you all power in return, does not compute.
   Powerlessness is one of the greatest weapons used in this battle against drugs and alcohol addiction. Becoming powerless also keeps us out of relapse mode! When people offend us, come into our space, disagree with us, powerlessness teaches us to let them be who they are. A person who thinks he has

power enters into relapse mode trying to control, direct, or influence other people's thoughts, deeds or actions.
Finally frustration gets the best of them, and they return to their old thinking, and they react the way they use to act when they were drinking and using.

In the beginning of your attempt to rid yourself of this disease of addiction you have to admit that you can not stop on your own. (No power) Next it will take a power greater than yourself (Jesus) to relief you of the pain, and suffering that you have been experiencing. Here the addict/alcoholic recognizes that he or she has no power to stop!

Next they recognize that God has all power! In the beginning we have to learn how to separate ourselves from the power we thought we had!

Paul explains it best in Romans 7:15 (New Living Translation) I don't understand myself at all, for I really want to do what is right, but I don't do it. Instead, I do the very thing I hate. (16) I know perfectly well what I am doing is wrong, and my bad conscience shows that I agree the law is good. (17) But I can't help myself, because it is the sin inside me that makes me do these evil things. Here Paul explains that he is trying to stop doing whatever it was he was doing, but he can't stop! Understand, this is a man who was starting churches everywhere he went. He also wrote 13 books of the bible. This is no ordinary man, this man knew the Lord well, and was a diligent worker for the Lord. But there was something that he was doing, and Paul describes it as a practice, and he surely could not stop on his own power. At verse (24) Paul says "O wretched man that I am! Who will deliver me from this body of death?" Paul is looking for help and it comes in the very next verse (25) Paul says, " I thank God through Jesus Christ our Lord!" Once the addict/alcoholic stops fighting this disease with their own power, and surrenders, God steps in and fights the battle for them.

Humbling yourself, denying yourself, receiving no glories, claming no power of your own and receiving all power!

Once you start practicing powerlessness in your life, you enter into the presence of almighty God. Here you are able to see God work miracles in your life, and the only possible explanation is that it was God that healed, fixed or changed, that situation.

So the question to ask is, how do you become powerless?

Humble yourself--even when you are right and you know you are right, give in to keep the peace. Give up your right to be right. Once you become powerless over people you allow them to be who they are! LET GO AND LET GOD!

Denying yourself--putting others needs before your own! Here you begin to develop a caring spirit. When practicing powerlessness, we do not have to be first any more, or be the best. This takes the pressure off us, and we can watch God work miracles in our lives as we help others. Don't get me wrong, we keep "pressing towards the mark of the high calling in Christ Jesus," but now that I am practicing powerlessness my mark has changed! Today I am seeking first the kingdom of God (serving others). So my goal is not to be first or the best, my goal is to serve God's people, and if God sees fit to elevate me to the first or the best, so be it!

Receiving no Glory--"don't believe the hype." Once God pulls you out of the hell that you were once in, after God picks you up and turns you around, once God begins to bless you financially, and opens up doors that were once closed to you, remember to give God all the Glory! People will pat you on the back and tell you what a great job you are doing, "don't believe the hype." You will take a look at your possessions, houses, cars, and money in the bank, "don't believe the hype." Promotions on jobs, successful ministries, "don't believe the hype!" All that you are is because Jesus died on the cross for your sins; and because we Love, Trust, and Believe in Him, God has given us power!

Understanding powerlessness also allows us to enter into acceptance. Acceptance gives us peace in the middle of the storm. We all ready know that we will be faced with trials and tribulations. The bible tells us so! So we have been fore warned!

In the Book of Daniel 3:19 - 30, the three Hebrew boys Shadrach, Meshach, and Abed-Nego were faced with a no-win situation (in the eyes of the world). King Nebuchadnezzar threatened to throw them into the fire if they did not bow down and worship his god. Powerless over this situation they accepted the decision that the king had made, and without worries, arguing, or fighting went into the fire. Because they accepted their fate and did not bow down because of the King's threats, God saw them through a horrible situation.

Today we are faced with our own personal trials. Trials that we have no control over, God shows all power in powerless situations. After the three Hebrew boys were thrown into the fire and the furnace was turned to its highest degrees, the Bible says King Nebuchadnezzar was astonished; and he rose and spoke, saying to his counselors, "Did we not cast three men bound into the midst if the fire?" They answered and said to the king, "True, O king." "Look" he answered, "I see four men loose, walking in the midst of the fire: and they are not hurt, and the form of the fourth is like the Son of God".

For example, your boss may tell you there is going to be a lay off or down sizing in your place of employment. A person who is not practicing powerlessness or acceptances will do everything in his power to stop this lay off from happening or he will worry until he takes a drink, or has a fix, or makes himself sick! Faith and powerlessness go hand in hand. We have to believe that God has another job for us!

Ronald Simmons

The day we start thinking we have power, over people places, or things, God has left the situation! And for some of us it takes another fall, or another bottom, to see we NEED Jesus!

Once again God allows us to be powerless! The one good thing about being on the bottom, once you are there, all you can do is look up!

Chapter Seven

THE RECOVERING ALCOHOLIC/ADDICT

The day you decide to surrender, and get help through the process, it is this day you become a recovering person. Here you will learn all kinds of tools to stay clean, and sober.

The recovering alcoholic/addict has to learn how to live a Christ-centered lifestyle. Going to, and participating in, meetings will be part of the process. Fellowshipping with saints, and getting a sponsor will be others. A sponsor is someone who has at least a year of any mind-altering substance. (See chapter on sponsor) This person has to be familiar with the 12 steps and the process of recovery.

The recovering person now entering this new life is at a very delicate point in his life! This is especially true for those who get involved in the Church! Recovering people are taught early in the process that their addiction is a disease, and that this disease rarely or never goes away. But it can be arrested. (See II Cor. 12:7-10)

When a recovering addict/alcoholic wakes up and recognizes that God has released him from this bondage of hell that he was in, a special bond is created between Jesus and the addict/alcoholic who had been doomed for death.

We in recovery know that what satan meant for destruction, God can use to his glory. Once an addict recognizes that he or she can not control his addiction or drinking, he is ready to begin his road to recovery. A person who totally surrenders listens as only the dying can! This person is ready for recovery when he recognizes, and fully understands that no human power can save him, and he suffers from a (3) three-fold nature, Mind, Body, Spirit.

1. The Mind --
   A. Is effected by our warped thinking. (Music sounds better when I am high)
   B. Will rationalize our condition, and what we do. (God made the weed, or coca plant, so it's OK)
   C. Is controlled by the drug. (Certain things will trigger the craving.)
2. The Body --
   A. Craves the drugs or the alcohol.
   B. Destroys the body.
3. The Spirit --
   A. Lacks spiritual connection.(Cuts his/her self off from God)
   B. Loses all moral values. (Does not care about anything)

In order for a recovering person to live a drug and alcohol free lifestyle, this person must first:
1. Learn how to take suggestions -- Walking in recovery is something new to the addict/alcoholic, and there are many people who have walked this path ahead of you; so, learn how to listen. And become teachable.
2. Be disciplined -- A recovering person must have his/her priorities in order and stick to them, no matter what!

3. Be willing to change -- When there is no change there is no change. You must be willing to change people, places, and things.

4. Not be willing to get well, but to get better. Always pressing towards the mark of the high calling in Christ Jesus.

Chapter Eight

UNDERSTANDING RELAPSE

Before I get started, I want to destroy a myth that seems to be floating around the rooms of recovery. This rumor is, relapse is a part of your recovery! For some strange reason people believe that in order to be free or participate in this process you must go out and drink or use over and over again. Always returning to the rooms of recovery to start this process again.

We know that people do relapse, and we thank God that there is a safe place to come and begin this process over. But it is not necessary to continue to fall. Once you read this, you do not have to practice your disease any more if you don't want to. In the Name of Jesus.

We know for a fact, that those who follow our path to freedom can claim freedom one day at a time! It is surely our goal that one day men and women will grab hold to this power that God is willing to give to all of us! All it takes is a made-up mind and a surrendered heart.

For those who relapse, our love for you is just as strong. We understand the disease of addiction, and we know that it is cunning, baffling and powerful. But we also know a God that has never lost a battle!

If you relapse, we beg you to get back up and try again. It is God's desire that every man be free from any and all kinds of bondage. As long as you have breath in your body, you have a chance to tap into this freedom!

For those who are applying this process into their lives, there are some things that you should watch out for!

Frustration--Because we no longer run from people, places and things, we have to be careful that we do not allow circumstances to frustrate us.

Boldness or Cockiness--When we start thinking we are normal, or well, and we don't fear the drugs or alcohol any longer, we are on the road to relapse.

Depression--Allowing situations, (that most of the time are out of our control) to bring us down. We start seeing that we are down more times than we are up! Call your sponsor - make a meeting and share about it.

Impatience--Wanting things to happen right now! Everything and everybody will not line up, and do what we want them to do, now that we are clean and sober.

Self-Pity--Because of life's difficulties, we tend to only focus on our own problems. We carry them around everywhere, and no one seems to care.

Ungrateful--forgetting where God has delivered us from, always expecting more.

Exhaustion--(A) trying to catch up with lost time, by becoming a workaholic. (B)Working through the process of recovery as fast as you can. (C) Believing you owe the people around you, so you volunteer for every project that comes your way. Make sure your priorities are in order! (list them)

Disobedience--Knowing right from wrong, but choosing to do wrong. Remember "God will not bless no mess"!

Forgetting What Got You Here – If it's not broken, don't

fix it. Meetings, Church, Checking in with your sponsor, prayer, Fasting, Studying the Word of God--These things help you obtain freedom. Don't abandon them!

Anyone who has crossed that fine line into alcohol and drug addiction is only one hit, or one drink, away from destruction. Always be on guard! I Peter 5:8 "Be sober, be vigilant; your adversary the devil walks about like a roaring lion seeking whom he may devour."

His main objective is to return you to drinking and using, and the pain that you once lived in.

Chapter Nine

WHY A SPONSOR

This question will always be asked, and has always been asked! Why do I need a sponsor? Why do I have to check in with someone, on a daily or weekly basis?

When Bill Wilson founded the 12 steps, Alcoholic Anonymous meetings began to spring up all over the nation and now all over the world. Since 1935, there has been few changes in the structure of AA meetings, in the Big Book of Alcoholics Anonymous, or in the love of one alcoholic helping another.

No one really knows when that first alcoholic, now with sober time, took a newcomer under his or her wings and said, "I will be your sponsor." Without the concept of "one addict helping another," Alcoholic's Anonymous, Narcotic Anonymous, Cocaine Anonymous, and Free N One would and could not survive. One addict helping another is therapeutic.

Recovering people tend to listen to people who have been through the muck and mire and come out clean on the other side. In the world of using, and drinking, the streets teach you not to trust anyone. In recovery we trust people with sober or clean time because, we are looking for someone to trust. Alcoholism and addiction isolate you from your family and friends, and you find yourself all alone, right where satan wants you.

Sponsorship really began in biblical days. During this time, they were called disciples. Webster defines a disciple as a pupil, or a bond by contract or other formal agreement.

When looking for a sponsor, we are looking for help. This help comes in the form of advice.

A sponsor's main objective is to:

1. Be a friend, and listen.
2. Guide the recovering person through the process, and the 12 spiritual ways to recovery.
3. Listen to the recovering person, and only suggest alternatives to the different situations that will come up in his day to day life.
4. Never co-sign the recovering person's addictive behavior.

What not to look for:

1. A person who wants to control your life.
2. A person who is too busy to spend time with you.
3. A person who wants to parade you around like a trophy.
4. A person who has not been through the process.
5. Do not let your Pastor, your good friend in the ministry, your family member be your sponsor. They cannot help you because they have no idea what the process of recovery is about. (Unless they have been through the process)
6. A person who is not a recovering person. (One addict helping another is therapeutic.)
7. A recovering person who is not practicing the process of recovery, and has more problems than you do.

What to look for:

1. A person who will not co-sign everything you say or do. This person must be able to tell you when you are right and when you are wrong.
2. A person who is focused on your growth, and not on perfection. As this person gets to know you, he/she will know what you are capable of achieving, and what you are not.
3. A person who is a coach and not a cop. He/she will encourage you to grow in your weak areas, and excel in your strong areas. The person will allow you to make your own mistakes, and when you do make them he/she won't condemn you.
4. Does this person have a sponsor? A person who has a sponsor humbles himself before men. This person is also teachable, and no matter how much "clean or sober" time he or she has is still willing to grow. We all have to be accountable to someone. No man is an island.
5. They love the Lord: if they love the Lord, they have moral obligation that they live by.
6. They are responsible: we look for order in their lives. If they are married, they respect the family institution. If they are going through trials in their marriage, they go through them with dignity. If they are single they are not playboys, or playgirls.

    I consider a sponsor, the same way I consider a mother bird taking care of a baby bird. She feeds him, she encourages him by way of example. Sometimes she has to hold him. Then one day, the mother decides that it is time for that baby to leave the nest. She picks the baby up and drops him out of the nest. It's time to fly. But the baby is always welcome to return and visit the nest.

We know that Christian recovery is new to most Churches, and congregations. In the beginning it will be hard to find sponsors. This will be one of your goals.

We suggest you pray and believe, and work the process to the best of your ability. God understands that you are new, and he will provide.

Ronald Simmons

Chapter Ten

THE CHURCH

For years the Church has been the first line of defense for a person who is suffering from this disease called addiction. The Church is always praying and caring for people who are consumed by this demon. In the 40's, and 50's, before anyone knew alcohol was a disease, the Church knew something was wrong. In the 50's and 60's, when satan attacked this country with marijuana, hallucinogenic drugs, and uppers and downers the Church was there. In the 70's, 80's and 90's, we are able to see satan's offensive plan of attack. Attack each major city and let the problem filter down to the suburbs and to the farmlands, until, there is not a place in this country that has not been effected by this disease, call addiction.

So what is the Church's counter offensive? It can be found in the Great Commission. Mark 16:15-18 (15)And Jesus said to them, "Go into all the world and preach the gospel to every creature. (16) He who believes and is baptized will be saved; but he who does not believe will be condemned, (17) And these signs will follow those who believe: In My name they will cast out demons; they will speak with new tongues; (18) they will take up serpents; and if they drink anything deadly, it will by no means hurt them; they will lay hands on the sick, and they will recover."

We in the Church know that, people are delivered from the laying on of hands. Unfortunately, some individuals in the Church believe this is the only way to recover. If this were so, we should be able to go to every state, to every city, to every dope house and bar and deliver men from their disease. Does God have another plan? Or does satan win this battle? God forbid! Believe me there is a "Ram in the bush."

It is a proven fact that some are instantly delivered by the laying on of hands, never to go and use again. Then there are other addicts/alcoholics who have the same hands laid on them and they turn right around and continue to be ruled by their disease. This person wants freedom just as much as any other person does, but for some reason does not receive deliverance. This person needs special counseling.

Let's take a look at those addicts/alcoholics who have hands laid on them and never go back to their addiction. What keeps them free, or what are they doing differently, that keeps them free?

We that work closely in this ministry have noticed one thing. The addicts/alcoholics that come to the altar and are completely delivered, surrender all. They are willing to give up everything! Not only the drugs and alcohol, but the cigarettes, the lying, cheating, stealing, and fornication. They are willing to give up their so-called friends and the whole life style! When freedom takes place, the power of God moves in them; and, in most cases, the desire for this lifestyle leaves as well.

Now on the other hand, addicts/alcoholics who go to that same altar, but return to using and drinking go to the altar just to be delivered from the drugs and alcohol. They are not willing to change their life style! God, who knows their heart, will not let freedom take place.

Because of a lack of education on the part of the Church and experience in the process of recovery, the Church has not been affective in this field. Even though the addict/alcoholic is thoroughly convinced he/she wants to quit, "want" is not enough to keep them free. Matthew 26:41 The spirit is indeed willing, but the flesh is weak! From the pew, to the choir stand, to the usher board, to the pulpit, untreated addicts/alcoholics are occupying churches all over the World. Two myths have infiltrated the Church:

1. He stops so he must be O.K. - Because he has stopped drinking and using for a few months, this does not mean he is healed. This demon will wait patiently until the unsuspecting person has his guards down, and then the demon will attack. 1 Peter 5: 8 Satan is like a roaring lion, seeking who he might devour.
2. "If we can just get them a job." - The answer to their problem is not a job. Most addicts and alcoholics have skills and are employable. The problem appears on "pay day" the day they receive their check.

Traditionally the Church will accept someone who has confessed that he has a problem with drugs or alcohol, and treat him with kid gloves. The Church, or someone in the Church, will take care of his immediate needs, which is OK! The problem begins when we continue to take care of this person and will not allow him to take care of himself, or trust God for himself. (Getting him a jobs, finding him a place to place to stay, making decisions for him, picking him up and taking him to Church, and bible studies) The Church enables this person, by not allowing him to stand up for himself. (Note: Every case is different, so you must use sound judgment. Like the mother bird that pushes that baby bird out of the nest, we must learn how and when to push!)

One of the biggest mistakes the Church will make, someone will tell this addict/alcohol that he is well. Now that the addict/alcoholic has accepted Jesus Christ as their personal

Lord and Savior, this does not mean they are delivered from their addiction. This is dangerous because this individual truly believes in the Church and believes what the Church is telling him. When he starts believing he is well, he stops going to meetings, checking in with his sponsor, and starts sociably drinking, and using. Once this happens, the disease of addiction is released. Just like any other untreated disease, it is alive and well, and will attack at any given time.

    We suggest a person should be free from their disease at least six months, before singing in the choir, or working on the usher board. A recovering person who is considering holding any office, such as elder or deacon, or ministering to anyone in the congregation, should wait a year. This gives this person time to find out who he is, and whose he is in Christ. It also gives him time to go through life's ups and downs without using or drinking.

During this time he starts building a stronger foundation in the Lord. (Remember this is only suggested.) In the past we have seen too many Christians with an untreated disease confessing before men that they are freed from their addiction, and somewhere down the line they secretly go back to participating in their disease. For those who are singing in the choir, working on the usher board, or sitting in the pulpit, the embarrassment is too great. Because of pride, they cannot tell anyone about this fall. Remember they have already confessed before men that God has set them free. So they try to hide their shame and guilt, until they can not hide it any longer. Most of the time they disappear from Church without a trace, only to reappear at another church to go through the same cycle. Some blame God, but most of them feel that they have let God down, or let the Church down. Some even believe that God is angry with them, because they have failed again, and they start believing that this freedom will never happen for them.

    The Church must learn how to be patient with that person who has just entered into this new walk called recovery! The

Church must give them time to grow up, before adding responsibilities to their lives.

So how do you work with a person who has been involved in the Church most of his life? He has sung in the choir, and been on the Jr. deacon board, and then on the deacon board. He knows everyone in the Church, and everyone knows him. He has taught Bible studies and led revivals. What do you say to a person who already has a personal relationship with God? How do you convince him that Jesus is the way to his freedom in Christ? He will tell you that he has been praying and fasting, going from one revival to another, attending all type's of healing service. He has been dipped in water, and covered in oil, but he continues to use.

The biggest problem with this type of addict is the same problem as with all other addicts, PRIDE! Their prideful ways make them harder to reach. First they have a hard time surrendering to anyone in the Church, because of the image they wish to uphold. So they keep trying to fool people until they cannot hide their addiction any longer. Second, it is hard for them to go to people in the Church because it was the same people in the church who told them they were free! And the last reason why it is so hard for the Christian who has been involved in the Church is he, himself, has been telling everyone he is free.

We tend to forget, that the Church should be a place where you can come and change your life. God forbid you should fall, but if you do, the Church should pick you up and walk with you again. I have interviewed hundreds of addicts/alcoholics who have been Christians for most of their lives. The first place they will look for help is a government-run rehabilitation program. Why? Because they know what the Church has to offer! They have done it before. It is time The Church take a look at the "Ram in the Bush!" God ordains this process of recovery. This process comes right out of the Word of God!

The Church should be the first place a person goes for help. And when he arrives, there should be a program in place that is highly successful. The Bible says at Matthew 11:28 "Come unto me all you who labor and are heavy laden and I will give you rest." Education is the key to the Church's success. From the pulpit to the congregation, we should understand the disease of addiction.

The Church should be a safe place for any addict/alcoholic to learn how to be free. But if they feel people are going to be-little them or talk about them behind their backs, why should they go! The bible also says at James 5:16, "Confess your faults one to another and pray one for another that ye may be healed. The effectual fervent prayer of a righteous man availeth much."

We teach the Church is a spiritual hospital where sick people go to get well. Most Christian addicts run from the Church because of shame, a sense of failure, guilt, or embarrassment. Most of them disappear from the Church, with their disease still untreated, and they live hopeless, letting the disease consume them.

Some addicts who come to the Church believing, if they get involved in an auxiliary this will help them. Remember this disease of addiction centers in the mind. An addict will quickly try to clean up the outside, and look good in front of people. For some addict/alcoholic, looking good or looking normal will be there reason for living. The outside may look good but the inside is still sick with the disease of addiction. So, Church leader be careful not to elevate this person too quickly. Make sure he is making meetings, applying the process of recovery in his life. You have every right to ask questions and be apart of his recovery.

For years recovering people that came out of secular programs such as Alcoholic Anonymous, Narcotic Anonymous, and Cocaine Anonymous were taught to refer to themselves as addicts/alcoholics. This was considered against

God's teaching in the Church, and they were told not to confess being an addict or alcoholic. The Church would take them to 2 Corinthian 5:17 "Therefore if anyone is in Christ he is a new creation old things have passed away behold all things have become new." Because this Scripture is not fully explained to the addict/alcoholic, most of them will hear this and try their best to live in freedom. When their disease overwhelms them, they leave the church embarrassed. They feel less than Christians, and defeated. Some even question if they are still Christians.

When we use 2 Corinthian 5:17 "Therefore if anyone is in Christ he is a new creation old things have passed away behold all things have become new." Teachers in the Church must let the recovering person know that Paul was talking about the spirit of man has become new! The flesh is still weak. It will take time for the flesh to catch up with this new spirit.

It is the recovering person's responsibility to replace the old with something new! And that something new is the Word of God, through the process of recovery. (Not just knowing the Word but living the Word of God.) This process of recovery is not going to happen overnight. It takes time to become new in the flesh, especially when you are working with alcoholics/addicts. They tend to hold on to the "old," because they are comfortable with the old. Even if the "old" almost destroyed them! We in the Church must understand that addicts and alcoholics did not become addicts overnight. The disease progressively got worse.

Addicts and alcoholics that have known God for years, and still seem to make it to Church every Sunday, have to deal with the embarrassment of the Church finding out. These people find it hard to come to that same Church and ask for help, because they were told they were new creatures in Christ. But they continue to use.

Still today one of the first places an addict or alcoholic looking for freedom from this disease is the Church. As the church comes together as one, equipped with knowledge and understanding about the disease of addiction, and the process of recovery, we will defeat this monster that is plaguing our communities.

If the Pastor supports recovery from the pulpit, their Church becomes a safe place for the addicted person. It becomes easier to ask for help when the Pastor shares from the podium, about God's recovery!

When the Church only teaches freedom and not how to get this freedom, the addict/alcoholic, hides in the closet, always wondering what is wrong with him?

Ronald Simmons

Chapter Eleven

WHY SO MANY MEETINGS?
THE MOST IMPORTANT PART OF RECOVERY! THE MEETINGS!

Working in Christian recovery brings a special challenge to most Christian counselors. The question always asked is why? Why do I have to go to so many meetings? Or can I just go to Church instead of the meeting?

In my early years working in Christian recovery, I used to think "yes you can substitute Bible studies for after-care, or Christ-centered meeting." So we allowed the recovering addicts or alcoholic to go to Bible studies during the week, instead of meetings. Our overall percentage of recovered addicts and alcoholic's cases went down drastically! Addicts and alcoholics began relapsing, and we had to admit them back into our in-house treatment program. Clearly we could see that this did not work. Quickly we changed our program back to mandatory Christ-centered meetings, where the percentage climbed back up. Here they could talk about, ask questions, and apply the process of recovery in their lives. Unfortunately, some things we had to learn by trial and error.

We found that because the addict and alcoholic is a very strange breed of people, they need special help. Concentrated meetings that deal specifically with their problems. Structured Christ centered meetings become a safe place to fellowship with people who are just like them. They can talk about and release all the demoralizing episodes of their past, and not have a fear of being judged. Some of these deep dark secrets are hard to share at bible studies. If these secrets stay hidden, satan has a way of allowing their past to haunt them and they will eventually return to using and abusing the drug or alcohol of their choice. One of satan's main tools is guilt. He will tell the addict or alcoholic that what they have done is not worthy of forgiveness. In most Christ centered meetings they allow the recovering person to confess their sins before men. When the newcomers hear this type of sharing, automatically their guards come down, and they, too, are able to talk about the pain that has been hidden for so long.

Here are a few more reasons why the addict or alcoholic needs their own meeting:

1. These meetings become a safe place because everyone there has probably done the same thing or something similar, so the fear of judgment disappears.
2. It's biblical - The bible says at Proverbs 28:13 He who covers his sins will not prosper. But whoever confesses and forsakes them will have mercy. (Psalm 32:5 – 1 John 1:9)
3. To get a recovering person to stand up and shares about the TV they stole from their family, the bike that they stole from their kids at Christmas, is not an easy thing to do. When they talk about being molested as a child, raped as an adult, selling their bodies for a hit, the brand new addict that walks into the room for the first time can feel free to let go of whatever is keeping him or her down. And in return they share, and for the first time they believe there is hope for them.

4. In the meeting there are other recovering addicts/alcoholics that understands the process of recovery, and are willing to walk with them through this process. (One addict helping another is therapeutic.

    The "sharing" part of the meeting is not only for releasing past sins, but it is also for dealing with today's trials. Most addicts and alcoholics have been running from responsibilities all their lives. Here they are able to talk about some of these trails, and get feedback on how to better deal with them. It takes a lot of courage to say "I have never worked on a job, so I don't know how to act" or "I have two kids and I don't know how to be a mother." Once again the meeting becomes a safe place for the now recovering addict or alcoholic who wants to grow.
    We believe that every Church should have some type of drug and alcohol ministry at their dwelling. If it's a meeting that will allow addicts and alcoholic from all over the city to attend, or someone on staff that is equipped to help the addicts or alcoholics in a one-on-one sitting. The Church should be a place where hurting people can come and receive special help!

Chapter Twelve

FREE "N" ONE

The drug and alcohol free program

Free N One – (free from drugs and alcohol and one in Christ.)

THE PURPOSE OF FREE "N" ONE IS:

1. To establish, provide and maintain inter-city drug and alcohol free meetings, centering in the Church.
2. To teach the addict/alcoholic how to be free, through the 12 Spiritual Ways to Recovery, and the Process of Recovery.
3. To establish a safe place for people who are addicted to drugs or alcohol and want to be free. (A safe place is a Church that will not judge them because of their illness.)
4. To educate the Church about the disease of addiction.
5. To provide help for the family and significant others through drug/alcohol support group meetings called Tough Love.
6. To assist the recovered addict and re-establish him back into the community by providing funds for continuing education or network for job placement.
7. To provide with other recovering people, so the addict can learn how to be free from his addiction.
8. To bring the Church together as one, to fight this affliction that is destroying our people, our cities, and our nation.
9. To educate the family member about codependency, and how to be free from the perils of the practicing addict/alcoholic. (Remember God gave you a life, are you living it, or are you taking care of the addict/alcoholic?)

In 1987, the founders of Free N One, Ronald Simmons, and now Rev. Ronald Wright, and Minister Rene Whitehead came together in response to a need. This need was a outpatient drug and alcohol program designed for the Church, rooted in the Word of God, led by the Spirit of God.

After weeks of meetings and months of planning, the founders established Free "N" One, the drug and alcohol free program. All three men, themselves, recovering alcoholic/addicts, had given their lives over to God, and noticed that something was missing in the care of the addict/alcoholic, and something had to be done. They recognized that the most powerful organization in the community (the Church) was silent concerning the disease of addiction.

They also knew that the only answer to this drug and alcohol problem is the power of God through the Church. One Church standing alone can not win this war on drugs and alcohol. It is going to take the whole body to defeat this demon called addiction.

Free N One brings each Church together with the same agenda, the same goals and objectives, all serving the same God! There is no one Church bigger or better than another. We all stand together in unity with one common goal, "Freedom" through Jesus Christ our Lord and Savior.

There are many reasons why we believe the Church should adopt Free N One. The most important reasons are that it is spiritually and clinically sound, and that it works.

Chapter Thirteen

12 SPIRITUAL WAYS TO RECOVERY

1. We admitted that we could not control our addiction and our lives became unmanageable (Romans 7:15-25)

2. Learned to believe that God can and will restore us to a right relationship with Him through Jesus Christ. (Matthew 11:28-30, Romans 3:22-23, Romans 5:9-10)

3. Made a quality decision to let God have complete control over our will and lives through His Word. Joshua 24:15, Psalms 119:4, Proverbs 3:5-6, Matthew 6:24, 33)

4. Made a thorough and fearless moral examination of ourselves on paper. (2 Corinthians 13:5)

5. Confessed to God in the name of Jesus and admitted to ourselves and unashamedly admit the exact nature of our wrongs to another human being. (Proverbs 28:13, James 5:16, 1 John 1:9)

6. Became entirely ready to have God take away all these blocks to our freedom in Christ. (Galatians 5:1, Hebrews 12: 1,2, Psalms 86:10-13, Psalms 119:57-59)

Ronald Simmons

7. Humbly asked God in the name of Jesus and thanked Him for His mercy and for giving us the strength to overcome our faults. (John 16:24, 1 Peter 5: 6-10, James 4:10, Psalms 51:10, Psalms 19:12-14)

8. Wrote down all those persons we had harmed and became willing to make restitution to them all. (Matthew 5:23-24, Luke 19:8-10)

9. Made direct restitution to such persons whenever possible except when to do so would injure them or others. (James 5:16 Luke 6:31, 36-37)

10. Examined ourselves daily to see if we are being doers of the Word and not just hearer only. If wrong promptly confess it. (James 1:22, James 5:16, 1 John 1:8-10, Ephesians 4:26)

11. Continue to pray, study and meditate on the Word, and maintain consistent fellowship with believers, to improve our relationship with God. (Joshua 1:8, Psalms 1:1-3, 1 Thessalonians 5:17, 2 Timothy 2:15, Hebrews 10:25)

12. Having had a born again experience and having been freed from our addiction we shared our testimony with those who are still in bondage and continued to be doers of the Word in all our affairs. (Matthew 28:19-20, Romans 1:16, Galatians 5:1 and 13, 1 Timothy 6:18, John 3:3)

Chapter Fourteen

12 SPIRITUAL WAYS TO RECOVERY

FIRST 3 STEPS GET YOU IN TOUCH WITH GOD

STEP 1

WE ADMITTED THAT WE COULD NOT CONTROL OUR ADDICTION AND OUR LIVES BECAME UNMANAGEABLE.

Step 1 is the beginning of recovery. If we can not admit that we have a problem, then we might as well go back to the pain and torment we were in. If we can not admit that our lives have become unmanageable, then we will never recover from this illness. People in denial are wasting their time, and the time of everyone involved. They must recognize their problem.

When an addict admits he or she has a problem, he has begun the most important act that he will ever do towards his recovery. For most of us, admitting that we have no power and no control is no easy task. No one plans to be an addict or alcoholic. No one plans to be separated from families and friends, and most of all separated from God! Once we get honest with ourselves, we realize something is very wrong. We have to allow God to guide us through this process called recovery.

Here at Step 1 we realize that we have no clue on how to stay clean and sober. We suggest that you take a very good look at your relationship with drugs and alcohol, and what it has done to you. When we began drinking and using, the trouble also began. Those who are honest with themselves and look back at this relationship with drugs and alcohol will see nothing but destruction.

Going to meetings, selecting a sponsor, and studying your Bible will be the first assignments asked of you on your road to recovery. Once we throw up the white flag and surrender, we must learn how to trust someone who has been through this process called recovery. Sharing with your sponsor and your new Christian friends will help you in growth during this first step. Honesty will be the addict's/alcoholic's next big hurdle. Like eating and sleeping, telling a lie goes hand in hand with using drugs and alcohol. Once we get honest with God and with ourselves we are on the road to freedom. For some it becomes easy. They recognize that they are on the bottom of this thing called life. Starting all over again, they begin their new life stripped of everything, unable to manage or hold on to anything. So they surrender, because they have tried everything else. From here all you can do is go up!

Then there are those who come into this process holding onto what little dignity they think they have left. It is not mandatory that you lose everything, but some of us do. But you must recognize that it is God and only God who can restore you to sanity. In some cases, not being stripped of everything can be a problem. Once the pain is gone, and you add a few more possession onto whatever you came into recovery with, it is easy to be tricked by satan, into thinking that you are not that bad. Unfortunately when you regain power, you loose humility. You end up using again and have to start this process all over again. When we humble ourselves, we understand that it is God who has spared us from losing everything, and it is God that will keep us free.

Also here at the first step you have to learn about the disease of addiction. We could tell you that every major medical association known to man considers addiction a disease. We would rather show you the disease in operation in the Bible.

This next scripture is one of the most powerful scriptures in the Bible, and it links powerlessness to what the addict/alcoholic goes through daily. What is interesting about this scripture, Paul the writer, was not a babe in Christ. By the time he arrived in Rome, 15 years had passed since his experience on the road to Damascus. He was a true man of God, yet this is how he felt!

Romans 7:15-25 Paul states (New Living Translation) (15) I don't understand myself at all, for I really want to do what is right, but I don't do it. Instead, I do the very thing I hate. (16) I know perfectly well that what I am doing is wrong, and my bad conscience shows that I agree that the law is good. (17) But I can't help myself, because it is sin inside me that makes me do these evil things. (18) I know I am rotten through and through so far as my old man is concerned. No matter which way I turn, I can't make myself do right. I want to, but I can't. (19) When I want to do good, I don't. And when I try not to do wrong, I do it anyway. (20) But if I am doing what I don't want to do, I am not really the one doing it; the sin within me is doing it. (21) It seems to be a fact of life when I want to do what is right, I inevitably do what is wrong. (22) I love God's law with all my heart. (23) But there is another law at work within me that is at war with my mind. This law wins the fight and makes me a slave to the sin that is still within me. (24) Oh what a miserable person I am! Who will free me from this life that is dominated by sin? (25) Thank God! The answer is in Jesus Christ our Lord. So you see how it is: In my mind I really want to obey God's law, but because of my sinful nature I am a slave to sin.

This is a classic example of what an addict goes through. Paul is controlled by/or addicted to some type of sin and is unable to stop doing what he is doing, under his own power alone. We thank God that Paul never told us what he was struggling with. If Paul had shared what this problem was, we would think that deliverance could only happen in this area. But in God's infinite wisdom, He did not tell us what Paul was going through. So now anyone who is struggling with any type of addiction can find freedom in knowing that a man who wrote 13 books of the Bible went through what they are going through now. So this section of scripture can apply to anyone who is having a problem stopping anything!

Satan does not care how strong you are or how much of a man you think you are; we all need God's Spirit to keep us from falling. And in the area of drug and alcohol addiction we need Jesus even more.

We must also remember that this is a spiritual warfare, and no matter what plan you try to put together, your fight will be fruitless. The Bible tells us in (II Cor. 10:3-5, For though we walk in the flesh, we do not war after the flesh: For the weapons of our warfare are not carnal, but mighty through God to the pulling down of strong holds; Casting down imaginations and every high thing that exalteth itself against the knowledge of God, and bringing into captivity every thought to the obedience of Christ.)

You can try to fight this battle on your own if you want to, but total freedom will be hard to come by. This is why some programs state "once you are an addict, you are always an addict."

Learning to be powerless will play a big part in a recovering person's life as he grows in recovery. Learning to be powerless means you are trusting in your whole life into God's hands, and He can do whatever He wants with it. The

Bible says at Isaiah 64:8 "Yet O Lord, you are our Father. We are the clay, you are the potter; we are all the work of your hand."

Here in the beginning, at step 1, a change must take place, and we must allow God to orchestrate this change. In our many attempts to rid ourselves of our addiction, our main goal was to stop using. Today we know that this can only happen when our thinking, our behavior, and Who we serve changes. One writer plainly put it, "When there is no change, there is no changes." If you do not change, you remain the same. Living the same way you used to live, doing the same things you used to do, yet expecting different results, is insanity!

It takes power to change, a power greater than yourself. If you could change yourself, you would not be in the predicament you are in right now!

The key to obtaining this power starts at becoming powerless. Powerlessness does not mean power will not be in your life. Power will come, but God will give it to you. So remember, it's God's power that lives in us! Not your power! The Bible says at James 4:10, "Humble yourselves in the sight of the Lord, and He will lift you up." Understand this concept, and you will continue to grow by leaps and bounds.

By the time we surrender here at Step 1, we are looking at an impossible situation. As you grow and study your Word, you will find out that God does His best work in impossible situations. It is almost as if God waits until we have exhausted every avenue. (Become powerless) Once we have no more fight left, God allows us to witness His power!

Powerlessness works in all aspects of a recovering person's life. It allows the recovering person to let other people be who they are. When operating in a powerless state, we learn that we can not control other people, places or things. We have to let people make their own mistakes in life, and allow them to live their own lives.

Ronald Simmons

We learn to be powerless over situations that occur in our own lives. This teaches us that things do happen, that are out of our control. In our addiction we got high or drank about life's situations. Today, because of powerlessness, we have learned how to take a deep breath, and use whatever tools we have acquired in this process, and not be mentally affected by life's situations. Powerlessness teaches us humility and patience, which helps us to think first before making any rash decisions, or running to our favorite drug or drink. Understanding the whole concept of being powerless allows the recovering person to live with peace in this new freedom that he or she has been blessed with.

Through God's grace, powerlessness allows the recovering person to witness Gods miracles, as they learn to step out of the way and behold the power of God!

Once a recovering person taps into this life of powerlessness, he grows by leaps and bounds in his recovery and his knowledge and respect for Gods power is increased!

STEP 2

WE LEARNED TO BELIEVE THAT GOD CAN AND WILL RESTORE US TO A RIGHT RELATIONSHIP WITH HIM THROUGH JESUS CHRIST.

After you understand the first step, you begin to apply this into your life, realizing that you cannot control this addiction, and cannot stop when you want to (once you realize there is no human power that can relieve you of the disease of alcoholism or addiction), and is time to be introduced to a Power that can free you from this dungeon called life that you are existing in. There is a Power that can free you, and that Power is Jesus Christ, our Lord and Savior.

Here at Step 2 you will begin your relationship with Jesus Christ. It is here that you will begin to understand His likes and His dislikes, and most importantly, how much He loves you. You will begin to discover these truths as you research the Word.

There are many ways to "learn" here at step 2. Everyone learns at his or her own pace, and in different ways, and God will meet you where you are. First you have to learn how to learn. We have to become teachable, reachable, and open-minded!

You must understand the difference between reading and studying. The Bible tells us at II Timothy 2:15 "study to show thy self approve unto God, a workman that needeth not to be ashamed, rightly dividing the word of truth."

Once you start studying God's Word, it will take you deeper into the heart and spirit of our Lord and Savior Jesus Christ. The Bible says at John 1:1 "In the beginning was the Word, and the Word was with God, and the Word was God!" Inside the Word, is God, and we understand God by, studying God's Word. The second part of this learning process is stepping out in faith, and doing some of the things that God has asked us to do in His Word. Here we have to "take action" or "participate in our own recovery!" Some things might be suggested by our sponsors, or our counselors, or by our Pastors. These things might be very foreign to you. For example, going to Bible studies, Free N One meetings, believing that this will work for you and you will get better. That's stepping out on faith!

Giving of your time, changing you friends and where you use to play is all a part of this learning process. This will take faith and courage on your part. Faith to step out, and courage to change.

Remember for the new person in recovery, you were doing your best thinking and you became a alcoholic/addict! Its time you take some suggestions! Here at Step 2 we begin the change from insanity to sanity. One writer's definition of insanity is "doing the same thing over and over again expecting different results." Here at step 2 we have to make up our minds to change, and to trust in other people.

When I first came through the program, I learned by watching other successful people go through this process. God works through people, and there is nothing wrong with that. Dr. Jeremiah Wright has a saying "It's OK to be a copy cat as long as you copy the right cat!"

As we begin to surrender our will, and accept God's will, we begin to see God working in our lives and that He has our best interest at heart.

Matthew 11:28 -30 says "Come unto me, all ye that labor and are heavy laden, and I will give you rest. Take my yoke upon you, and learn of me; for I am meek and lowly in heart: and ye shall find rest unto your souls. For my yoke is easy and my burden is light"

Here God calls everyone who is loaded down with any kind of burden (drugs and alcohol addiction) to bring those burdens to Him. God wants our problems, our pains, and our sickness. We must learn how to turn our lives over to Jesus.

We must turn doubt and fear into trust and faith, and study the Word of God so we will know what, God the Father has in store for us.

Once you begin to "Try God" you will see how much God loves you! When we were practicing our disease, we turned our back on God! One writer wrote, "we left God, God never left us!'

Joshua 1:5 "No one will be able to stand up against you all the days of your life As I was with Moses, so I will be with you; I will never leave you nor forsake you."

Some of us come to God battered, beaten down and confused, without any hope, some worse than others. The only person who can pick you up, dust you off and restore your hope in yourself is Christ Jesus.

Learn to believe that God can and will restore us to a right relationship with Him. Develop a personal relationship with the Lord. Know God for yourself. Pray morning, noon, and night, and God will reveal Himself to you.

Working in this ministry, I have found that some people just have a hard time believing in God. Some were brought up never going to church, or were just never introduced to God in any way. For these addicts Step #2 is where they get stuck, and eventually this is where they return to their drug of choice. They have a problem with some of the things that they have read or heard. Jesus walking on water, or God parting the Red Sea. Most of these people will not say that He did not do these things, but they will not say God did them either.

I have two suggestions for these addicts/alcoholics:

1. Sincerely ask God to make Himself real to you. In time God will reveal Himself to you.
2. Think back on the times when you escaped danger, and the only reason that you are alive today is because of a miracle! Some of us have been shot, cut by knives, been raped, kidnapped, or have overdosed on drugs. Some of us drank

so much that we have experienced black outs, not knowing what happened, where we were or who we were with. Waking up safely at home, not knowing how we got home, or where we were the night before. Sometimes it seems as if our cars automatically drove themselves home.

Some say it is luck, but we who have come to believe that God can do all He said He could, do know that it was God's Grace that watched over us. (Even in our addiction) It was God's Grace that kept us.

Once God has revealed himself to you, you must work on developing a personal relationship with God. This work is never ending. Until Jesus comes back or until we die, we must continue working on perfecting our relationship with God. For example on the day before Martin Luther King was killed, He shared something with the world that I will never forget. In one part of his speech he said, "mine eyes have seen the Glory of the coming of the Lord!" Then he went on to say, "I may not make it to the mountain top with you, but as a people we will all make it to the mountain top! At that time everyone thought this was just another great speech. Martin was killed the very next day. He knew he was going home to be with the father. What type of relationship did he have with God?

Philippians 3:14 "I press towards the mark for the prize of the high calling of God in Christ Jesus." Always striving to better your relationship with God.

STEP 3

MADE A QUALITY DECISION TO LET GOD HAVE COMPLETE CONTROL OVER OUR WILL AND LIVES THROUGH HIS WORD.

Making a quality decision means, having a made-up mind to follow God, and living the Word of God to the best of your ability. Making a quality decision means not only making God our Savior, but making him Lord of our lives. Once God is Lord of our lives, we bow down before him in awe of His Love, His power, His presence. At Step #3 we have made up our mind to trust God!

Matt 6:24 says "No man can serve two masters, for either he will hate the one, and love the other; or else he will hold to the one, and despise the other Ye cannot serve God and mam'-mon." (Or money)

The practicing addict/alcoholic Christian, in the church, will frequently find themselves straddling the fence. They will go to Church on Sunday, but find themselves drinking and using and caught up in worldly activities, from Monday to Saturday.

Some practicing Christian addict/alcoholic choose this lifestyle. They believe that God won't mind them having one foot in the world and one foot in faith. They struggle for years trying to make this lifestyle work for them.

On the other hand there are some practicing Christian addicts/alcoholics that continue to run to the Church for help! Deep down inside they know that God can! Even though they have been living in sin all week, they know deep down inside that their help comes from God! As their disease progresses they slowly disappear from Church. The guilt and remorse separates them from God and they hit a bottom quickly.

Step 3 for the recovering addict is a giant step. Anyone who decides to apply this step into his or her lives will never regret it. Saying "yes" to God, no matter what. And learning how to say "no" to the world.

Here at step 3 we concentrate on giving God our whole day every day "ONE DAY AT A TIME." Here we set time apart every day for the Lord, through prayer, meditation and reading God's Word. At step 3 we have made up our minds to, not just be a hearer of God's Word, but a doer of God's Word. Here at step 3 we begin to live as Christians. (Christ-like)

Those who believe that this is a hard step, refuse to surrender to God totally. They believe they can skip this step and reap the benefits, by working the rest of the steps. Those who choose to skip, or avoid or leave Jesus out of their recovery, seem to go through life searching for victory. Even though they are free from drugs and alcohol they continue to try and fill a void that can only be filled by Jesus. Peace, joy and love seems to elude them as they look for these things in all the wrong places.

The recovering Christian individual has to make up his/her mind to live for God, or continue using; there is no in-between!

I have to admit, if there ever was a scripture that did not set well with me early in my walk with God, it was John 8:32, and it reads "You shall know the truth and the truth shall make you free." Working with Christian addicts and alcoholics, I began to question this scripture. How can you know the truth and be a junkie or an alcoholic? Some of the people that were coming to me for help have known the truth all their lives! Some grew up in Christian families, some could quote scripture from one cover of the Bible to the other. They knew the truth, but they could not stay free from drugs or alcohol. I actually avoided this scripture, because I was meeting too many Christians bond to drugs and alcohol.

Deep down in my heart I believed all the stories in the Bible. Jesus walking on water, God parting the Red Sea, or

Jesus raising Lazarus from the dead! But I had a problem with "You shall know the truth and the truth shall make you free!"

After studying God's Word I finally got my answer! The word "know" in this sentence means to "live" in the Greek translation. Now this makes sense! You shall "live" the truth and the truth shall make you free! Anyone who lives the truth will be free! You're not "living" the truth hanging around those old so-called friends. II Corinthians 6:14 "Do not be unequally yoked together with unbelievers. For what fellowship has righteousness with lawlessness? And what communion has light with darkness?" It is impossible to live the truth spending week nights in nightclubs, chasing the opposite sex, or justifying drinking a beer, etc. etc. Some of us have deep-rooted habits that are hard to break. But we all know right from wrong. The problem with Christian addicts/alcoholics is they would rather live wrong.

Living wrong is not an option for us any more. Living wrong separates us from God. Once we turn our back on the truth, we enter into relapse territory.

Understanding patience, asking for forgiveness and repentance will be the key to our walk back to God's Power.

1. Patience – Not beating yourself up for being a babe in Christ and/or making mistakes.
2. Forgiveness – Forgiving yourself for mistakes and believing God has forgiven you!
3. Repentance – Learning to turn away from those things that God hates.

Everyone makes mistakes; no one is expected to be perfect. If you fall during this walk, (God forbid), get up and ask for forgiveness and continue your walk. Get back up and continue doing what is right in the sight of the Lord.

Remember satans job is to lure you back to him by any

means necessary! He will use anything and everything possible. Things like frustration, depression, and failure have turned many recovering people away from God, and back to the old life style.

Galatians. 5:1 says stand fast therefore in the liberty where with Christ has made you free, and be not entangled again in the yoke of bondage.

Ephesians 6:13-14 (NIV) says Therefore put on the full armor of God, so that when the day of evil comes, you maybe able to stand your ground, and after you have done everything, to stand. (14) Stand firm with the belt of truth buckled around your waist, with the breastplate of righteousness in place.

Psalms 46:10 says be still and know that I am God! Sometimes we have to get out the way and watch God work.

No matter what happens, we have to learn how to trust in God, and believe "everything is going to be all right."

I am convinced that if you accept Jesus Christ as your personal Lord and Savior, and believe in your heart that, God raised Him from the dead, heaven is your home. If you make a quality decision to let God have complete control over your will and life, you can have heaven right here on earth. At the same time there will be those that accept Christ into their lives, but still straddle the fence. They will make it into heaven, but they will have hell right here on earth! These will always wonder, what's wrong with them? For the Christians, "GOD WILL NOT BLESS NO MESS." If you decide to turn away, or play games with the truth, God has many ways to get your attention. Some addicts want to live a lukewarm lifestyle in Christ, then wonder why they are having so many problems. Revelations 3:16 "So, because you are lukewarm, neither hot nor cold, I am about to spit you out of my mouth."

Making a quality decision means you spend quality time in prayer, and meditation, and studying Gods Word. We must make a quality decision daily. Daily we must learn how to give our lives to him. This is a continued practice, until Jesus comes back.

Luke 9:23 "If anyone would come after me, he must deny himself and take up his cross daily and follow me." (One day at a time!) Deny those things that you use to do, or still want to do!

Here at step 3 we are not asking you to walk on water, we are asking you to step out on faith and begin living right in the sight of God. We know that this is new for most recovering people, so easy does it. Just like when you were out in the world and you had separated yourself from God, God was still with you. How much more will God be with you now that you have turned your life over to Him.

Ronald Simmons

Step 4

MADE A THOROUGH AND FEARLESS MORAL EXAMINATION OF OURSELVES ON PAPER.

REMEMBER THE 4TH AND 5TH GO TOGETHER

In order to carry out a successful 4th step, first you must fulfill a quality 3rd step! We have found that those who avoid the 3rd step, run from, or have a difficult, 4th step.

Let's define the key words in the 4th step before we start.

1. Thorough -- complete; extremely attentive to accuracy and detail; painstaking.
2. Fearless -- without regard of consequences; bold.
3. Moral -- conforming to accepted or established principles of right conduct; upright; virtuous; honest.
4. Examination: -- inspection; inquiry; investigation. Medically speaking -- to evaluate general health or determine the cause of illness.

Most people ask why a 4th step? This is asked by 95% of all addicts/alcoholics that have ever walked through the doors of recovery. Why do I have to bring up all that pain?

Many people fight with all their might when they get to the 4th Step. Some are afraid to open up and face their past? Which they have been covering up for years.

Some Christian addicts/alcoholics will use scripture such as II Corinthian 5:17 "Therefore, if anyone is in Christ he is a new creation; old things have passed away and behold all things become new." Their argument is, if they are "new," why do they have to go back in their past?

What Paul was saying in II Corinthians 5:17 is, yes you are a new creation. But new in your spirit. When we walk through the doors of the Church, our flesh, our thinking, our ways, are still the same! It will take time for you to be a "new creature," in your flesh. Take an honest look at yourself, examine yourself, and find out who you really are! The fourth step is design to reveal is some of those fleshly behaviors that will hinder our walk with God.

Another scripture that is always used is Philippians 3:13b "but this thing I do, forgetting those things, which are behind, and reaching forth unto those things which are before."

Yes, we believe you have to forget those old things in your past, but first you have to identify them.

For years addicts and alcoholics have been running from these haunting memories. Every time they catch up with us, we medicate ourselves with the alcohol or drug of our choice, or the sin of our choice. (Sex, illegal activities) Never knowing why we have returned to the substance of our choice, or to that behavior that always gets us into trouble.

We find that the 4th step is not only spiritually sound but clinically sound as well. Psychologists tell us we, as people, hold on to or cover up too many things that have happened in our past. Things that we suppressed or tried to forget. If we do not release them in a positive manner, they begin to build up like a boiling pressure cooker. This pressure cooker can explode at any time, and sometimes over the smallest things. Once this happens we return to what is easy for us, using drugs or alcohol.

Deep-rooted memories begin to show up, of rape, child molestation, child neglect, loss of a love one, and physical and mental abuse. These memories are magnified in a person's life and are easy to see in a 4th step. Sometimes triggers are not so noticeable. They can sometimes be many small events or not so noticeable behaviors. Things that are subtle, things that you would never consider as being the reason why you drank and used! A broken heart, a broken relationship, not knowing your father or mother, being sensitive and hurt by insensitive people.

Losing a loved one and blaming it on God, low self esteem, and depression; these are just some of the things that can make a person return to drinking and using, or to his old behavior. These things come out in a 4th step, if you are honest, fearless, and thorough.

Some try to stuff feelings, only to have them surface years later. Some drink and use drugs, and others overeat, just to name a few ways to escape. As their past begins to catch up with them, and satan floods their minds with the things they did or things that happened to them, some even commit suicide as a way of escape.

We know that it is impossible to run from yourself. One writer wrote "everywhere you go, there you are." For an addict/alcoholic this is especially dangerous. This disease can be triggered at any time. Without any apparent reason an addict/alcoholic will go out and practice his or her disease. And when asked why, after years of being free from drugs or alcohol, the addict/alcoholic will tell you "I just don't know why." Ironically they really don't know! They don't understand this is a disease that consumes them. They don't know that something in their past is tearing at their spirit, causing them to drink or get high! This may be the only honest thing they have said in a long time! Truthfully they really don't know.

It is vital that the recovering person completes a 4th steps. You may not see it now but the freedom you will experience will make your walk with Christ, a joyful walk. You will be able to move freely in Christ, and in your day to day walk. You will not be afraid of your past, and you will not allow it to effect your future.

There are several reasons we specifically ask you to write down these things on paper.

1. You cannot rely on your memory in dealing with these problems. You must sit down and write these things on

paper. Once they are on paper we learn to confront our past and learn how to put it behind us forever.
2. We also found that there is a release, and an escape like no other, in writing a thorough and fearless moral examination on paper.

How do you write a 4th Step? Where do you start? Do I write about myself my family? These are some of the questions we are asked by recovering people who arrive at the 4th Step.

Here are several different ways to actually write a 4th Step. First it is very important that you write a 4th Step with someone who has been through the process and has written a 4th Step!

This person should be someone that you trust someone who will not co-sign your excuses, or look down on you because of your past. This person should also be someone that will not join in your pity-party. If you share it with someone who does not understand the disease of addiction, or who does not understand the process of recovery, that person could make you feel worse than you felt before you began this 4th Step.

One way to write a 4th Step is to just sit down and start writing your life history, noting the good with the bad as far back as you can remember. Take each member of your family and write as much as you can on only this family member and your relationship with him. It must be in-depth, detailed, and thorough. You must write down, if you like him, if you love him, if you dislike him or hate him and WHY! If you do not address the why, you are wasting your time! When writing a 4th Step, you do not have to finish it in one sitting. Most sponsors will guide you through each family member, or each situation, until you are finished. (Remember you must finish.)

STEP 5

CONFESSED TO GOD IN THE NAME OF JESUS AND ADMITTED TO OURSELVES AND UNASHAMEDLY ADMITTED TO OURSELVES THE EXACT NATURE OF OUR WRONGS TO ANOTHER HUMAN BEING

Step 4 and 5 go together

It's no accident that after you have written down all these things in your 4th Step, after you have faced all your fears and resentment, after you have written down all these demoralizing things on paper, here at Step 5 you must confess to God, and to another human being.

The very first concept that you have to understand is Confession. Coming in Jesus Name is the second. Let's take a look at #2. How to approach Jesus! For many practicing addicts/alcoholics (this writer included) when we found ourselves in trouble we would call on God at the drop of a hat! If we were standing before a judge who had our lives in his hands, or if we were caught in a dangerous situation because of some of the choices we made. The most famous prayer ever said by most addicts/alcoholics after drinking and using for weeks at a time, destroying everything and everyone that gets in our way. Tired of getting high, tired of not being high. Tired of being up all night, and tired of seeing the sun come up in the morning, just tired of being tired! Finally we have hit a spiritual, and mental, bottom; we cry out "God will you please help me!" God because of His Grace and His Love for us, picks us up, cleans us off, and heals our wounds again. (Rescued!)

I have discovered many recovering people (this writer included) coming into the Church, not knowing that God has made it very plain and simple how we were supposed to come to Him. John 14:6 "Jesus answered, "I am the way and the truth and the life. No one comes to the Father but by me." The recovering person must understand that God sent Jesus here to be mediator between us and all mighty God. The only way we can get to God is through his Son, who is Jesus Christ. This is the reason we end all prayers "In Jesus' Name."

The first part of Step 5, confessing to God and another human beings, and believing that God has forgiven us all our sins. It is time to give all the pain, all the hurtful events in our past that use to haunt us, to God. The same God that took us out of that hell we once lived in wants to love us back to sanity. He wants to introduce us to peace.

We have already learned at Step 2 how to turn it over to God! We know that recovering people beat themselves up more than anyone else. More than our Mothers and Fathers, more than our Loved one's and friends. We find a secret place and cry until there are no more tears. Never letting anyone no the pain we are in.

Even though you have finished your 4th step, satan's job is to test your faith. Do you really believe God has forgiven you? Psalms 103:12 say's "as far as the East is from the West, so far has he removed our transgressions from us." A concerned sponsor or Christian friend will continue to remind you of God's Love for you! The Bible also says at Romans 4:7 "Blessed are they whose transgressions are forgiven, whose sins are covered. Blessed is the man whose sins the Lord will never count against him." Here God's Word consoles us. All those negative things we did in the past have been forgiven. We are blessed because the sins are many!

The 3rd part of Step 5 is: Unashamedly admit the exact nature of our wrong to another human being. James 5:16 "Confess your faults" one to another, and pray one for another, that ye may be healed.' The effectual fervent prayer of a righteous man availeth much."

Every psychologist in the field of counseling today uses this verse of the Bible. Once you walk into a psychologist's office the first thing he/she will have you to do is sit down or lie down, and talk about what is going on with you. Here at James 5:16 after we have confessed one to another God is asking us to also pray for one another (this is something that most psychologists will not do) that you may be healed. Healed from what? Healed from the pressures of life, that seem to pull us down daily. Healed from the wrong decisions that we make daily, and have made in our lifetime. Healed from the guilt that we carry around, but try to hide, or healed from our past that continues to haunt us! Here is a perfect example of God working through other people.

Once we start sharing, and praying with other people, they can stand in agreement with us as we walk this road of recovery. Satan's job is to remind us of our past sins. He wants to trick us into believing that we are not worthy of being free, or of being Christians. Our sponsor, our friends that we have shared 4th Step with, can remind us, which we have already confessed that sin to God, so why are we still carrying that sin around?

Bishop Charles E. Blake shares a story about a man who knelt down at the altar for prayer. As the Man of God prayed for everyone on the altar, and told them to cast all their cares upon God for He cares for you, the man at the altar down on his knees knew that the Man of God was talking to him. As the Man of God finished the prayer, everyone on the altar rose and headed back towards their seats. Suddenly the man who was on his knees turned around and went back to the altar, picked up all those cares, and burdens that he had left, and returned to his seat. This is a classic example of an addict/alcoholic having a hard time letting go.

Unashamedly: not ashamed, without guilt, without doubt. There are two reasons why we unashamedly admit to another human being. (1) So we can keep our heads up high because we know where we were before God rescued us. We also know that He loves us and that He has forgiven us. (2) You will find that one day your past will help someone else.

Confessing our faults/sins every night before the Father is something we must do before our heads hit the pillow. As you grow, you will learn to confess during the day! And never forget, end every prayer **"IN JESUS NAME."**

Step 6

BECAME ENTIRELY READY TO HAVE GOD TAKE AWAY ALL THESE BLOCKS TO OUR FREEDOM IN CHRIST.

Once you have finished your 4th and 5th step, this picture of the real you start's to become clearer. With the help of your sponsor, and or concerned Christian friends, you will start to unfold some of these character defects and defense mechanisms that came about because of your drinking and using.

Step 6 prepares us for taking an honest look at ourselves. It let's us know, now that we have accepted Christ into our lives, and have taken a good look at ourselves, we see something's that we do not like. In our make-up there are some behaviors that must be dealt with.

When we crossed over from darkness into His marvelous light, we brought most of our garbage (defects of character), if not all of our garbage, with us.

Some of these defects of character have been practiced so long that they have become spirits! Things like, disobedience, resentments, anger, laziness, lying spirit, being unforgiving, gossiping, backbiting etc., etc. Motivated by pride and selfishness, these things block our freedom in Christ.

As we slowly begin to take steps in the Lord, we should always be striving to be the best person in Christ that we can be. The Bible says, Philippians 3:14 "I press toward the mark for the prize of the high calling of God in Christ Jesus." We know that some of our character defects can hinder our walk with the Lord, especially when God has revealed these defects of character to us.

For the addict/alcoholic, a change in our behavior is a must because, satan will use our old behavior to take us back to that bondage that God has set us free from. Here at step 6 we must become "entirely ready"; or be willing to take an honest look at these defects of character. If we do not attempt to change these defects of character, we will find ourselves year after year in the same spiritual place with the Lord. Always wondering why everybody around us is growing spiritually, and we are not. Consequently, other faults appear, such as jealousy and bitterness. Satan has managed to take our eyes off the Lord once again.

Psalms 51:10 states, "Create in me a clean heart, Oh God; and renew a right spirit within me." This is a great prayer to remember as we grow, and walk in the Lord.

Remember this change will not come overnight so "Easy Does It," but "Do It." Even recognizing each character defect does not happen overnight. One step at a time, one defect at a time!

We thank God that He does not reveal all these defects of character to us at once. That would be unfair to us, and most recovering people would not be able to handle what we really look like to God. Another reason why God gives us one defect at a time, is because to see all of these defects of character would overwhelm us and we would, believe this task to be too great. This is why it is OK to be a babe in Christ. Revealing everything at once could leave this person worse off than when he entered. (Remember God will not give you any more than you can handle) So if God reveals this character defect to you, it is your responsibility to change it.

Here at step 6, God is not finished with you. We, as recovering people, should want to do our best to please God. Working on ourselves will be something that we will have to continue to do until Jesus comes back.

Step 7

HUMBLY ASKED GOD IN THE NAME OF JESUS AND THANKED HIM FOR HIS MERCY FOR GIVING US THE STRENGTH TO OVERCOME OUR FAULTS.

After recognizing your faults its time you do something about them. Yes! All of them! The first word in this passage is humble. (Humble -- not proud or haughty, in behavior, attitude, or spirit:) This is one of the most powerful words in the bible, and for recovering people one of the hardest behaviors to acquire. If we take a look at its opposite "Pride," we see that "humble" is Godly, and "Pride" is evil. It was pride that got satan kicked out of heaven. Isaiah 14:12-15. "Because he exalted himself, he was doomed to the lowest hell!" Jesus greatest act of humility is that He humbled Himself at the cross, and laid down His life for us! All through the Word of God Jesus pleads with us to humble ourselves.

Like satan, while we were in our disease we were caught up in pride. Even though the warning signs were all around, we did what we wanted to do. Most of us knew right from wrong, but we chose to do wrong.

Humility plays a big part in our recovery. Learning how to be humble will be a life-long task.

I Peter 5:6-10...(6) "Humble yourselves therefore, under Gods mighty hand, that he may lift you up in due time. (7) Cast all your anxiety on him because he cares for you. (8) Be self-controlled and alert. Your enemy the devil prowls around like a roaring lion looking for someone to devour. (9) Resist him, standing firm in the faith, because you know that your brothers throughout the world are undergoing the same kind of sufferings. (10) and the God of all grace, who called you to his eternal glory in Christ, after you have suffered a little while, will himself restore you and make you strong, firm and steadfast."

The Bible says in 1st Peter 2:1-3...(1) "Therefore, rid yourselves of all malice and all deceit, hypocrisy, envy, and slander of every kind. (2) Like newborn babies, crave pure spiritual milk, so that by it you may grow up in your salvation, (3) now that you have tasted that the Lord is good."(NIT) Here Peter is telling us to get rid of all these things that we brought into the kingdom when we accepted The Lord Jesus into our lives.
Let's take a look at some of them:

1. Malice -- the desire to see another suffer, or the intent to commit an unlawful act or cause harm without legal justification or excuse.
2. Deceit -- the act or practice of deceiving, misleading, trick, not truthful. One speaker notes "Once you tell a lie God has left the conversation."
3. Hypocrisy - Actor, being something that you are not, pretending to believe what one does not.
4. Envy -- Not liking someone because of what they have or what God is doing in their lives.
5. Slander -- the utterance of false charges or misrepresentations that defame and damage another person's reputation. Be a stumbling block to someone.

We have to start craving for the spiritual milk like a newborn babe. We know that this milk will make us healthy and strong. Verse 3 says "now that you have tasted that the Lord is Good" I didn't get high today; the Lord is Good; I'm not out of my mind today; the Lord is Good; I'm not sleeping on the street today; the Lord is Good. My family is back in my life today," the Lord is Good." "I have a reason for living today" the Lord is Good!

We should come to the Lord with a humble spirit. Remember God is getting ready to change our lives if we allow Him. There is one thing about God, He will not make us do anything. We have to make an effort to change. If we learn to take one step, God will take two for us.

In the Name of Jesus who is the King of Kings and the Lord of Lords we ask God to take these defects of character from us.

John 16:24 "have ye asked nothing in my name: ask and ye shall receive, that your joy may be full."

Step 7 goes on to say "giving us the strength to overcome our faults." We need this strength, because there are something's that are deeply embedded in our psychic, or our mental make up. Unfortunately these behaviors make us who we are. Some things we do not want to let go of, even after we recognize them. This shows us another defect of character, and that is being stubborn and selfish.

In Step 6, we come to grips with these things. In Step 7, we start working on these things.

The bottom line is, everything we do, every prayer we send to God, we humbly do it in the name of Jesus--always thanking Him for His mercy, and giving us the strength to over- come our faults; so we may become those Christians that God would have us be.

Step 8

WROTEDOWN ALL THOSE PERSONS WE HAD HARMED AND BECAME WILLING TO MAKE RESTITUTION TO THEM ALL

Step 8 and Step 9 go together

Here at Step 8, we prepare ourselves by writing down, the names of all those people we have harmed in our addiction.

This step is important, because during our insanity we hurt so many people, and neglected so many responsibilities-- not paying bills, not being the mother or father that we were supposed to be, neglecting ourselves, and burning bridges with our loved ones, family and friends. Sometimes it is hard to believe that there is any hope in restoring our lives, let alone our relationships with others. We have found that if we pray and fast God can work a miracle in any situation. In most cases people will love and respect us even more.

After we start on the road back to recovery, and God has forgiven us all our past sins, and wiped our slate clean, it is time to make an effort to mend some of those bridges we have destroyed.

This is where we humble ourselves, and start writing down the names of those people that we have harmed. This is not a time to write down what some of our loved ones did, or have done to us. Most of the time they are retaliating, or responding, to something that we have done in the past. If we can get honest, we will see it was our addictive behavior that caused most of the problems.

We must understand that in some cases people will not forgive us, because the pain is too severe. What we will be attempting to do is reconcile, by praying and fasting about each family or loved one, and each situation. Attempting to clean up your past is all-apart of being responsible. This is what God would have us do. Proverbs 28:13 "He who covers his sins will not prosper, But who ever confesses and forsakes them will have mercy. "

Even if people do not receive you well, you have done what God wants you to do, and God honors it and recognizes what you have done. There is healing in doing what God wants you to do.

This is not an easy step, when you have written down these names, you must pray, fast and meditate, and be willing to ask for forgiveness at the proper time. Be ready, because God will put some of these people or situations back in your life, so you may be healed, and grow. Watch God work a miracle in your life.

Step 9

MADE DIRECT RESTITUTION TO SUCH PERSONS WHENEVER POSSIBLE, EXCEPT WHEN TO DO SO WOULD INJURE THEM OR OTHERS

Step 8 and Step 9 go together

In Step 8, we have prepared ourselves, and recognized the people that we have harmed. In Step 9 it is time for action. When God puts these people or situations, in your path, there are two things you can do. You can avoid the person or situation or you can address the person or situation in order that you may grow.

What does the Lord say about restitution?... Leviticus 6:1 (NIV) "The Lord said to Moses: (2) If anyone sins and is unfaithful to the Lord by deceiving his neighbor about something entrusted to him or left in his care or stolen, or if he cheats him, (3) or if he finds lost property and lies about it, or if he swears falsely or, if he commits any such sin that people may do-- (4) when he thus sins and becomes guilty, he must return what he has stolen or taken by extortion, or what was entrusted to him, or the lost property he found, (5) or whatever it was he swore falsely about. He must make restitution in full, add a fifth of the value to it and give it all to the owner of the day he presents his guilt offering." (NIV)

Today we seek forgiveness, from the people that we have wronged. In some cases we may have to restore in full, the cost of the property we took. But in most cases our love ones will be happy to see that we are attempting to straighten our lives out, by being honest with them.

When you go in the name of Jesus, there is nothing to be fearful of. God is with you, and he knows you are doing the right thing. Isaiah 41:10 "So do not fear, for I am with you; do not be dismayed, for I am your God. I will strengthen you and help you; I will uphold you with my righteous right hand. (NIV) "

Caution: Some people and some things you will not be able to address. Some people, because of the severity of the situation, might injure you, or others. You may have to keep this one between you and the Lord. For instance, adultery--you cannot tell another person that you had an affair with his spouse. This could not only harm you, but his spouse as well. USE WISDOM!

Step 10

EXAMINE OURSELVES DAILY TO SEE IF WE ARE BEING DOERS OF THE WORD AND NOT HEARERS ONLY. IF WRONG, PROMPTLY CONFESS IT.

Step 10, 11, and 12 are maintenance steps.

James 1:22 says "But be ye doers of the Word, and not hearers only, deceiving your own selves." Here at step 10 you get a tool that helps you in your daily walk. Examine....To inspect closely, to inquire into carefully, to test by questioning in order to determine progress.

Take a good look at yourselves daily to see if you are following God's Word. For us as recovering addicts/alcoholics it is easy to fall back into our old behavior. Honestly examine yourself. Are you going backward, are you going forward, are you standing still. `Philippians 3:14 I press toward the mark for the prize of the high calling of God in Christ Jesus. God forbid anyone find themselves going backwards in their walk with the Lord. For an addict/alcoholic this surly means relapse. One of God's goals for every Christian is to go higher in Him.

Those that stand still get caught by the enemy, which is always looking for someone that has gotten complacent in their walk with God. The Bible says at 1 Peter 5: "Be sober, be vigilant; because your adversary the devil, as a roaring lion, walketh about, seeking whom he may devour." Those that stand still get caught!

We must examine ourselves daily to see if we are living the way God would have us to live. John 8:32 says you shall know the truth and the truth shall make you free. The words "know" in the Greek translation means to live, or recognize truth by personal experience. Living God's truth every day is our goal. We know we cannot be perfect people, but in Christ we keep striving to be the best Christians that we can be. It's sad to say that today there are too many hearers in the body of Christ, and not enough doers.

There would not be as much pain in the body, or in the world today, if there were more doers of the Word.

In our everyday life it is so easy to be led astray and caught up in worldly or fleshly ways. The Bible says at Matthew 7:23 "Enter through the narrow gate. For wide is the gate and broad is the road that leads to destruction, and many enter through it. But small is the gate and narrow the road that leads to life, and only a few find it. Those who seek the Lord will find the way."

During our meditation or quite time, before we get on our knees, to ask God to forgive us our sins, we should think about our day. Think about how we handled different situations, where we fell short. We need to ask for forgiveness, and understanding of how we could have handled these situations better. Our goal is to become better Christians, and it will take searching our *own* selves, and honestly examining our actions and re-actions and doing our best to live better!

Step 11

CONTINUE TO PRAY, STUDY AND MEDITATE ON THE WORD, AND MAINTAIN CONSISTENT FELLOWSHIP WITH BELIEVER, TO IMPROVE OUR RELATIONSHIP WITH GOD.

Most addicts/alcoholics relapse when they stop doing the things that got them clean or sober in the first place. An addict will get 6 months, 9 months, 1 year, 2 years, 3 years, of clean and sober time, and for whatever reason, some will stop praying, stop studying the Word, stop fellowshipping (going to 12 step meetings). Soon they find themselves back practicing their disease, getting high, even more often than before. The Bible talks about unclean spirits coming back to a dwelling they use to live in. Matthew 12:43-45 says, "When an unclean spirit goes out of a man, he goes through dry places, seeking rest, and finds none, (44) Then he says, "I will return to my house from which I came." And when he comes, he finds it empty, swept, and put in order. (45) "Then he goes and takes with him seven other spirits more wicked than himself, and they enter and dwell there; and the last state of that man is worse than the first. So shall it also be with this wicked generation."

For the addict/alcoholic that is involved in this process, you cannot afford to get well, or thinks that you have arrived, or think you are normal. Satan's job is to deceive you into thinking you do not need to continue making your meetings, studying your Word and fellowshipping with the saints. When you stop, you actually stop taking the medicine for your disease. Satan's job is to steal, kill, and destroy, your life.

Our direct line to the Father, through Jesus, is prayer. God is waiting to hear from us. God is our Father and we are His kids, and God wants to develop a personal relationship with us. Luke 22:40 "Pray that you will not fall into temptation." Matthew 26:41 "Watch and pray so that you will not fall into temptation."

IT'S A MUST THAT WE CONTINUE TO PRAY

We have to study to understand Gods character, to understand his righteousness, to understand what God has for us. We must continue study to understand life, love, grace, humility, peace, joy, happiness, right, wrong, etc. By studying Gods word we grow in him. The bible says, II Tim. 2:15 "Study to shew thyself approved unto God, a workman that needeth not to be ashamed, rightly dividing the word of truth."
Did you know that there is a difference between reading and studying? There is also a difference between studying and living! The Bible says Hosea 4:6 "my people are destroyed from a lack of knowledge."

STUDY THE WORD OF GOD

Hebrews 10:25 says, Let us not give up meeting together, as some are in the habit of doing, but let us encourage one another---and all the more as you see the Day approaching. (N.I.V)
Here we see where fellowship is important. The 11th Step means fellowshipping with people just like you, recovering addicts/alcoholics. Meeting people in 12 step meetings is a very good place to meet people just like your self. Getting involved in Church activities and Church auxiliaries, is also an excellent place to meet new Christian friends.

We suggest 3 meetings a week, one Bible study and Church on Sunday. Now you may think that this is a lot, but remember you got high every day. It's going take to every day to restore you to sanity, and to develop a right relationship with God.

MAKE YOUR MEETINGS, FELLOWSHIP WITH BELIEVERS, STICK WITH THE WINNERS

Step 12

HAVING HAD A BORN AGAIN EXPERIENCE, AND HAVING BEEN FREED FROM OUR ADDICTION, WE SHARED OUR TESTIMONY WITH THOSE WHO ARE STILL IN BONDAGE AND CONTINUED TO BE DOERS OF THE WORD IN ALL OUR AFFAIRS

Have you ever asked God, why He saved your life? Or why was He watching over you while you were using and abusing drugs and alcohol? Or have you ever asked why did He protect you while you were locked up in jail, or caught in a dope house with no money? Or the question I had to ask myself, why did the bullet miss me? Or if it hit you, why are you alive today? If you have not asked yourself this question, then maybe you should ask!

I had to ask God why me? Why spare my life? Some of us not only turned our backs on Christ, some of us worked for satan. We sold dope, we turn people on to dope, and God turns around and saves our lives! You have to ask yourself "what type of love is this?"

Now that you have arrived at this 12th step, and God has only begun to restore order back into your life, it is time to give back what so freely was given to you! Who can better share with someone that wants to be free from drugs and alcohol than you! God saved you for a reason, and that reason is to tell someone that is bound by this disease, how they can be free.

Sometimes I wonder how God looks at a person that He has set free from drugs or alcohol addiction, and this person gets involved in the Church and never tells anyone what God has done for him. Why? Is it you don't want anyone to know that you were a dope-fiend, a junkie, or maybe you were a drunk, an alcoholic. The most important word in both those statements is "were"! We pray that you will take time out and think about the pain you were in. (there's that word again) How can you act like you never went through this period in your life! I am sure if they were still adding pages to the Bible, some of our stories would be in there.

We have a saying in this process called recovery "I was saved to serve" bottom line! You cannot be blessed with this freedom and keep it to yourselves. Too many of Gods people are dying. We beg of you, never forget where you came from. Somebody needs to hear your story. Tell somebody in bondage just what God has done for you. After you have shared with them, be a committee of one, and take them to a Free N One meeting. (Each one teach one.) Once God has taken you from the pit of hell, picked you up, and cleaned you up, God expects you to share with others, especially those who are suffering from drugs and alcohol addiction.

For some reason, some people think that what God has done for them, (delivered them from drugs and alcohol) He was supposed to do! No! It was the GRACE of God that saved you.

What we have received from God is a modern day miracle. This miracle is just as big as God parting the Red Sea, or Jesus walking on water. It's equally as significant as Jesus raising Lazarus from the dead. Matter of fact we were dead, we just hadn't laid down yet! We cannot take for granted what God has done for us! We should be excited about this modern day miracle that has happened in our lives.

Some people ponder over what ministry they should pursue, or pray about what field they should be involved in, and rightfully so. Maybe you want to sing in the choir, join the usher board, or maybe join the evangelist team. Well, you should be apart of these ministries, especially if there is no drug and alcohol ministry in your church. (God forbid) There is nothing wrong with it, but you should never stop telling people what God has done for you!

To keep what God has done for you a secret would be a sin! Addicts and alcoholics that have been rescued by the power of God should yell it from the mountaintop, and let everyone know that it was God and only God who saved their lives!

One way to do this is to attend many meetings. Not only will you be helping yourself, but you will be helping others who still do not believe, or struggling with this process. There are a lot of newcomers at the meetings, and they need to hear and see other delivered addicts in the meetings, sharing about there experiences, strength and hope!

Matthew 9:37-38 Then Jesus sayeth unto his disciples, The harvest truly is plenteous, but the laborers are few; (38) Pray ye therefore the Lord of the harvest, that he will send forth laborers into his harvest. You are part of that harvest!

Continue to grow in the Lord. One of the biggest problems with being free from drugs and alcohol is that we tend to get well, and we forget where we have come from and what kind of person we used to be. Remember the disease of addiction centers in your mind. And as long as you can remember, the disease of addiction is with you.

Humble yourself at all times, the thorn in your flesh is still there. As you humble yourself, God will give you strength to share everywhere you go. Stay willing. Stay open. Not only will you be a blessing to someone else, but God will bless you also.

This is a motto that I live by: **I WAS SAVED TO SERVE !**

Chapter Fifteen

FREEDOM TOWERS

For years I have asked God to show me how to explain this process of recovery in a way that everyone would be able to understand it. After years of teaching and sharing this process called "recovery" with addicts, alcoholics, loved ones, and the church, I knew deep down inside people still didn't fully understand, God finally answered my prayer.

Each process is different for each individual, all I ask is you go with me as I share with you, what God gave me.

Bear with me as I do my best to paint a vivid picture of the process of recovery in action.

It all begins in a 12-story building called the process. Each floor in this building represents one of the 12 spiritual ways to recovery. Here at the process many are given an opportunity to get their lives together. Some accept the challenge, and move on from floor to floor. Some decide not to go on this journey, and they stay trapped in their disease. Those who continue traveling from floor to floor learn more about God, themselves, and how to be what God has called them to be. They also learn about the disease, and how it has affected their lives and everyone around them.

Most people who start this process have tried every avenue to get some stability back into their lives. They always seem to fall short of their goal, of total freedom. By the time they make it to the doors of recovery, they are spiritually, and mentally, and physically bankrupt. Most addicts/alcoholics have to hit a serious bottom before they surrender. There are two good things about hitting a bottom:

Ronald Simmons

1. There is no fight left in the individual. Surrendering to the process becomes easy.
2. Once a person is on his bottom, all he can do is look up!

BASEMENT

Here at this 12-story building, recovery starts in the basement. People in recovery call it "hitting a bottom." In this basement there is much pain, tears and confusion. Everyone here at the basement wants help. Some want it more than others, but for sure everyone here needs help. Some people have been here before, but because of a lack of effort, or missed information, they return to start this process again. Unfortunately for some strange reason, some stay on the bottom and accept, or surrender to, the environment that they are living in. On the bottom confusion runs wild; people are doing whatever it takes to survive.

ON WITH THE JOURNEY

At some point each person is given a chance to get off this bottom. People in recovery call it a moment of clarity. Unfortunately for some, it is only a moment! At that moment you must take advantage of it. It is at this moment, God is giving us an opportunity to save our lives.

It's like throwing a lifeline out to someone who is drowning. There is nothing you can do if the drowning person does not reach out and grab the line.

In the basement of this building, this "moment of clarity" shows up in the form of an elevator. Suddenly a light comes on above this elevator. The light is an arrow pointing up! Once the doors open, some jump on quickly, some get on reluctantly, and some walk to the door and turn around. It is a fact that addicts/alcoholics have a fear of change.

Ronald Simmons

First Floor

THROW UP THE WHITE FLAG!

Once you step onto the elevator, a sign reads "To make it to the top you must Trust and have Faith in God." At that moment some people begin to panic! All through the elevator people are whispering things like, "How do you Trust in God?" or "Who is God?" "What is Trust?", "What is Faith?"

As the elevator slowly inches its way up to the first floor, a voice comes over the intercom. "Do you believe that this elevator will take you to the floor that you desire, without any hurt, harm or danger? If so then you are putting your faith, and trust, into something that you know nothing about, but you enter the elevator anyway!" A sense of peace falls on everyone. Once again, the voice says "Be still and know that He is God!"

It is at this time I started thinking about the pulleys, and the motors that allowed this elevator to rise and fall. I thought about the cables that kept this big steel box we are riding in from falling back to the bottom. For some strange reason, I just automatically believe it will take me safely to my destination!

Slowly the elevator comes to a complete stop and at this point I know that this is going to be different from any thing that I have ever experienced. Once the doors opened, we all stepped off onto the first floor.

Directly in front of us was a sign that read "follow the arrow to the room called SHARING." On the wall was a large red arrow that led us down a hallway that was painted white. As we all entered into this room called "SHARING," there are chairs lined up in rows, a chair for each person. After we were all seated, a person came out wearing all white. He began to share his experiences, strength, and hope with us. He talked about how he lived before he entered recovery. He also talked about the changes he had to make to be a new person today!

One thing he said that I would never forget was "When there is no change, there is no change!" Next he gave us an opportunity to express ourselves, and share about our feelings. He told us that if we did not share what was inside us, then these things could build up inside and cause us to relapse. After we finished, there were tee shirts folded neatly on a white table near another doorway. A sign above the table read, "Put tee shirt on before moving on!" After we put the tee shirts on, the writing on the shirt read, "God will never leave you nor forsake you!"

As we walked through this room with our shirts on, we entered into a large opening. In this opening there were many doors that must be opened in order to move on to higher floors! Behind each door there were separate rooms, and in each room there are tools inside that will help you understand your recovery.

The first room we walked into was entitled "Powerlessness." In this room were our own individual doors. Once I opened the door and walked in, I found myself standing at the "start" line on a race car track. At this start line, there were 3 of my favorite automobiles, Targa Porsche, Lamborghini, and the Corvette. Whoever put this room together knew me very well, because I love fast cars. Another person in a white suit said, "You have 25 seconds to drive one of these cars 100 yards across the finish line. If you can do it in 25 seconds, that car will be yours. Starting right now!" I thought to myself, no problem. I ran to the Lamborghini and got in. I reached for the keys, and there were no keys. In the background I could hear the seconds being counted down 21, 20, 19, I got out of the Lamborghini and dashed to the Corvette. The seconds continued to count down, 17, 16, and 15. I reached for the key, turned it, nothing happened, 13,12, out of the Corvette. I ran to the Porsche 10, 9, 8 seconds. I still have time. I reached for the key and turned it; to my surprise it started up. 8 - 7, I threw it into gear and it went dead, 5 - 4 - 3 -2 - 1. Everything disappeared and I found myself standing in the room again outside the door. I thought to myself, " what a cruel trick, what was I supposed to learn from this?"

Before I could think about it, I was led to another room. Once I walked through the doors, I was led to a booth that had a set of headphones in it, and a chair. As I sat down there were instructions on the wall that read:

(1) Put headphones on.
(2) Push "On" button.
(3) Hold on!
(4) Don't leave 5 minutes before the miracle.

After I turned the headphones on, I could not believe what I was hearing. Things like "You are an addict, and will never be anything but an addict." Harsh things like "your daddy was nothing so you will never be anything." It seemed as if it would never end, the things I heard through these headphones! I heard that I was a liar, a cheat, and that I could not be trusted. It said that I was too black and too tall, and that I would never amount to anything. Ten minutes of this madness was nine minutes too long. Right before I was ready to snatch these headphones off, a calm voice started speaking. This voice said," You are powerless over what other people think, write and say about you". Here I must learn that there is "power" in being powerless. It takes power and strength to hear things like this and not allow them to move or change you, or divert you from your primary purpose. Never again will I allow things that others say affect me. (Unless they are true; then change must come!)

On this first floor I must learn how to be Powerless over people, places, and things." If I don't, I am doomed to repeat my insanity again! Here on this first floor, I learned that you cannot control anyone but yourself.

I was led back into the "sharing" room. Here I met my friends that I started this journey with. They all looked as they had been through something just as shocking as what I had gone through.

We were all led into another room filled with chairs where we all took a seat. A speaker came out and shared about being powerless over his addiction. He shared it did not matter how strong we thought we were. We were powerless over our addiction. It all began to make sense. I had had an opportunity to own or at least drive some of the most powerful cars in the world, but because they had no power, they were nothing but beautiful shells, going nowhere.

So it did not matter how big I was, how smart I was, how much money I had. I had no power to fight this disease called addiction. If I could fix myself, I would not be in the position that I was in right now. Here I learned that I needed a power greater than myself to restore me to sanity.

Another thing I learned was, knowing that I am powerless is an advantage! Every day that we practice powerlessness, we are learning that God has all power and we should humble ourselves, and submit to Him. It sounds easy, but for some people old habits are hard to break and they never grasp being powerless.

The next room on the 1st floor is called "Willingness". The door to this room led us to an opening on top of a hill that overlooks a valley. There was a very narrow path that led down into the valley that disappeared into a jungle of trees and shrubbery. A heavy mist hovered over one part of the valley; this looked like a lake of some kind. Strange sounds came from deep within the jungle. The sky was gray, and some very large birds circled overhead. As we began our journey down into this thick bush, some hesitated and decided that they did not want to go. We tried to talk them into coming with us, but they were afraid and turned around and went back through the door. Once we got closer to the thick trees, there was a sign at the edge of the forest that read "do not go down this path, please take that path".

We followed this path to another door that led into another room. In this room there were chairs for us to sit. Once we were all seated, a person came out and began to share her experience, strength and hope. She also shared that, now we were in recovery we had to start trusting someone. We also had to be willing to go to any length to be free from our addiction. She said that we who were willing to go down into the valley had passed the test and understood the word willingness. We were ready to move on to the next room.

Here in this room called "Willingness," all you have to do is be willing. If you learn how to take one step God will take two for you! In this room called "willingness," things are going to be foreign to you. You will have to do some things even when you do not want to do them or understand why you are doing them, like attending meetings. But you must learn how to change! As we began to leave this room, we saw a glass partition on the wall behind us. Here we could see people on the other side, but they could not see us. We noticed some of our friends who had decided not to follow us down into the valley. Some stood at the door called "Willingness," afraid to go in. As I looked through the glass, I could see their t-shirts which read "God will never leave you or forsake you". I thought to myself, "this is what trust is all about".

As we were led down this hallway, we came once again upon a table with tee shirts on it. The sign above the table read, "Take one and put it on." The inscription on this shirt read, "**DO NOT LEAVE 5 MINUTES BEFORE THE MIRACLE.**"

Walking out of this room, I believe we all questioned what we had gotten ourselves into! But so far it was better than where we had come from!

The next room is entitled "Honesty".

Ronald Simmons

Once we walked into this room, we all noticed about 15 doors that led into other rooms. We were all led to one of these doors. As I got closer to my door, I noticed my name on the outside of the door. As I walked into this room, lights came on and to my surprise this room was set up just like my apartment. (But cleaner!) Everything was in place. From the pictures on the wall, to the sofa, the kitchen, and the den, were all the same. As I walked into the bedroom, my TV and stereo system were in the same place. This was starting to feel weird, like something out of the twilight zone. As I walked in front of my bedroom mirror, I noticed the writings on my tee shirt that said, "do not leave 5 minutes before the miracle". It took me a while to get used to, but soon I began to settle in and move around this apartment freely!

Finally I noticed one thing that was different! There was food in the refrigerator, and in the cabinets. After eating and enjoying a little cable TV, I decided to turn in. After all it had been a long, and somewhat unusual day! After dozing off I fell into a deep sleep. I began to dream about "young adult" days. It started off when I graduated from high school and college. It took me back to my first touchdown pass that won the game that beat our rival school. It also took me to the first home run I hit in a baseball game, and how all these different colleges wanted to recruit me. Next this dream took me to my college years where I partied and stayed in nightclubs all night long. Picking and choosing all the women I wanted. It moved on to the days when I was selling dope and making big money, and meeting important people! Hanging out with the rich and famous crowd, and how they were glad to see me when I showed up!

After waking up and having breakfast, I began to think about this dream and this "honesty" room I had entered. I tried to put everything together but nothing made any sense. After breakfast, I turned on the TV and I could only get one station. On this station there were some instructions for me. They instructed me to sit in front of the TV. Then they instructed me to pick up the remote control. It was different from any other remote. On this remote there were only four buttons. One was "power on", one "power off", and the other two were "true" and "false." I hit "power on," and the TV went to a white screen. It began to play my dream back. It showed me graduating from high school and then it paused. The words "True" or "False" flashed on the screen. I pushed the button "true", and the story of my life began to move. Next it stopped at graduating from college and paused again. "True" or "False" flashed on the screen, and I pushed the button "true." The screen began to flash "False - False."

I remembered that I really did not graduate from college; I was a few credits short. I had been living this lie for years. So I hit the button "false" and the story of my life began to move again. It went back to the days when I played football. It was the final game of the season, and I caught the pass that won the biggest game of the year. "True or False" and I hit "true." Once again "False -- False" began to light up on the screen. As I sat back and got honest with myself, I realized I had been living another lie! I had never caught a winning catch, nor had any colleges recruited me. I wasn't this big time ladies man at the nightclub. In fact I really depended on alcohol to have my way with women. Slowly, in every area of my life, bubbles were being busted! I wasn't this big time dope dealer. Truthfully I was a small time hustler trying to make a dollar, and ended up a junkie becoming my own best customer!

Once this was all over, and my ego had been smashed flatter than a dime, a sign on the TV screen read "TO THINE OWN SELF BE TRUE" "TO THINE OWN SELF BE TRUE." As I sat back in my chair, feeling low enough to play handball against the curb, a voice came over the TV and started to explain why honesty was so important. It said, "Here in the honesty room, if you cannot be honest with yourself, how will you be honest with God! Remember you are on the first floor.

This is the beginning, and you do not want to start this process of recovery off living a lie! Those who try to continue living this lie and participating in the process are known as "FAKES, PHONY, FRAUDS." Going through the motions of being free. Struggling through life, never enjoying peace, joy, and serenity. Some return to the pain and suffering that got them there. To these we say "Good Luck" instead of "Be Blessed!"

As I headed for the door to exit this apartment, there was assign on the door that read, "Who is the real _____" (put your name in here). After thinking about this question for a few minutes, I couldn't come up with an answer. I put my head down and walked out of this fake apartment and closed the door behind me. I looked down the hallway and I noticed my friends coming out of their doors at the same time.

All of us seemed to have the same look on our faces. Like we'd been in a 12 round fight with the heavy weight champion of the world. As we were led down this long hallway, it was so quiet you could hear a pin drop. It gave us a chance to think about, the time we had wasted, trying to be something, we were not.

Again we were led to the "sharing" room. This time it seemed easy for us to share, because we needed to "dump" all the garbage that we had been carrying around with us for years. While listening to everyone who went before me, I realized I had not heard such sincere, and heart sharing, in all my life. I was only on the second floor, but I knew that I was going in the right direction.

We were all led to what they called the "Living Room." In this room we were allowed to live the changes we had learned on the 1st floor. Minimum time on this floor is 1 month. For some it takes longer.

Second Floor

EDUCATION

After spending a month in the "living room," I decided to move on to the second floor, convinced that what I had learned on the first floor would be with me for the rest of my life.

Once we entered the elevator, and the doors closed behind us, a voice came over the intercom that said, "Remember the road to recovery is a process, and complete healing will not come overnight. It took years to reach the position you are in. So it is going to take some time to be restored to sanity!"

A sign on the elevator door read: "Those who try and hurry through this process without using these tools tend to repeat "this process" by returning to the bottom." (These are called chronic relapser's)

Once we exited the elevator onto the second floor, we walked right into a world filled with books. The hills, and the mountains, were filled with books. The trees, the leaves were made of books. Everywhere you looked books! As far as the eye could see, there was nothing but books. Every book that had ever been written must have been here in this world of books.

Far off in the distant, which looked like the center of this world of books, we could see a beam of light, shinning down in one specific area. We all decided to head towards that light. As we began this journey through this land of books, we were allowed to pick up and read any book of our choice along the way.

After about a day's walk we came upon a fork in the road. At this fork there was a sign that said "each road leads to the light." At this fork, there were many roads that seemed to go in many directions. There was a street sign on each road, describing it. One sign said "disease of addictions," one said "codependency and enabling," and another said "recovery" and still another said "powerlessness." At the bottom of the sign, it said "you can return at anytime and choose another road." I, along with a few other people, selected the road called "disease of addiction," and still others went their own way. After we said our goodbyes, we started down this road called "disease of addiction." Soon people in our little group started finding and picking up books to read. Soon I noticed a book that caught my eye. It was entitled "Addiction Is It a Cancer?" Once I picked up the book, another book with the same title appeared in its place. After we all found a book of our choice, we each found a tree and began to read our books. I was amazed to find out that my addiction was considered a disease. I learned that in order for me to rid myself of the craving this disease produced, there were some things I would have to do. This book also taught me that this disease centered in my mind, and it was going to take a process called recovery to renew my mind. It was almost like brain washing. As I sat there and thought about all the stupid things that I did, and all the wasted time that was spent, my brain needed washing! For some reason I just thought I drank and smoke too much. This book explained to me that I wasn't a bad person trying to be good, but a sick person trying to get well. Who knew!

Once we finished our books, we continued our journey towards the light in this land of books. After a couple of days, reading and a walking, we finally arrived at the spot where this light was shining down so brightly. As we got closer, it seemed to draw us to it, and we could see all the roads in this land of books leading to this light. Our other friends who had selected other roads were arriving at this light at the same time. Once we arrived at the point where the light hit the ground, we could see that it was landing on one particular book. THE HOLY BIBLE!

Everyone stood in line and picked up a Bible, and just like the other books, another Bible appeared in its place. Once I picked up my Bible something inside me leaped on it. There was truly something very special about this Book! After all of us had retrieved our Bibles, a person in a white suit came out and began to tell us the story about Jesus. For 3 weeks this person walked with us through the Bible. We were encouraged to continue studying the Word of God and to seek growth in our lives.

As we were led out of this room, to the room called "SHARING," a woman came out and shared about morals, truth, righteousness, and holiness. She also shared about this Book called the Bible and how it changed her life once she surrendered to it. Her testimony was powerful because she was just like me, and she made a decision at a crossroad in her life, and decided to go with God. After she finished, a man came out and shared about being teachable, and being willing to change. He said that changing was going to be our biggest battle. I thought about the road ahead. From bad to good was not going to be easy, when I was so use to being bad. I knew my biggest challenge was going to be in the area of changing. Education about this disease and knowledge about my Lord and Savior were the keys to my recovery and this change. After he shared, we all got a chance to share and talk about what we had been introduced to so far on this floor. After everyone had finished sharing, the speakers advised us to return to this room at any time during this journey. They also told us that before we move to the next room we had one more room to enter.

We were all guided to a large room with many doors. The word "FAITH" was on every door. We were all led to a door and were instructed to go in at anytime. After a slight hesitation I turned the doorknob and entered. Once inside, the door closed behind me and I could not see anything. I ran my hand along the wall searching for a light switch, but I could not find one. Afraid to move, I stood there for a while wondering should I turn around and go back, or should I just stay here and wait. Finally, I took a step into the darkness, and when I did, to my surprise a light came on under my feet. So I took another step and another light came on. With each step I got bolder, and lights began to shine all over the room! After a while all the lights were on inside this room. On the other side of the room, there was a door that led outside into another area. Above the door there was a sign that read "Faith is an action word. You must step out into nothing to get something."

After leaving this room, we all met in the room called "Sharing." Once we had taken our seats, the speaker began to share about studying God's Word, and how knowledge was power. He shared with us that the steps, that we had taken, took a lot of faith, and courage, and that we were like babies in this new walk with God and recovery. Then he asked us to share. I was amazed to hear how many people felt the way I was feeling. A little bit scared, but willing to go on. Not afraid of what we were learning but, because this new life was so unpredictable, sometimes hesitant to move on.

It was time to move on to the next floor. Before we left the speaker reminded us that none of the doors, we had to face could be opened without the tools we had received on the first (2) two floors. Then he said there was no time limit in acquiring these very powerful tools, but without them we could not proceed, or we were destined to fall. Then he said, "once you feel comfortable on this floor, you can move on to the next floor. Please take your time in this process called recovery. It took years to get sick; it's going to take time to recover!"

We walked down the hall towards the elevators that would take us to the third floor. We were surprised to see there were individual elevators for each of us. They were going to separate us! Some people faces showed fear, but we were reminded about our journey on the second floor. God would never leave us or forsake us, this kept ringing in my soul. I also thought about what I learned in the Faith room -- stepping out into nothing to receive something! And what about the Willingness room, I have to be willing to change. So we all said our farewells and we all entered our elevators.

Third Floor

SURRENDER ALL!

When the doors opened on the third floor, there was a huge welcome sign that said, "Welcome To The Third Floor." As I walked out of the elevator, there was one big giant door. This door was not like any other door that I had witnessed. This door was made of gold and marble. It stood 50 feet high, and was laced in diamonds and pearls. Just looking at this door, I thought there was no way I would be able to open it. There were no instructions on the walls like the other floors had. There were no doorknobs and no doorbells.

Suddenly a person, in all white, appeared. He told me I had to make a decision about turning my life over to God, and if I said yes, it would be the best decision that I would ever make. He also shared that many people say "yes" with their lips, but to understand and receive the full impact of what God has to offer, you must say it with your heart. He went on to talk about the phony's that come to God looking for a quick fix, and because He is God, He already knows their thoughts, and their motives. Then he talked about the difference between God being "God in your life" and God being "Lord over your life." Once God is Lord over your life we bow before Him in awe, doing whatever He would have us to do. He then grabbed my hands, as tears rolled down his face and said, "Make his heart a clean heart O Lord and change his ways." He then asked me "if I was ready to make a quality decision to let God have complete control over my will and life! I looked at him and said "yes"!

By faith I started toward this magnificent door. With every step I took, the doors slowly opened.

As I walked through the doors of this room, suddenly I was standing at the top of a small hill, overlooking a valley. Down in this valley were hundreds of beautiful trees. A large sign at the edge of the valley welcomed me and called this valley the "hiding place." Under this sign was a huge stone tablet, with letters engraved in stone. The inscription explained and described everything in this beautiful valley. First I noticed the large field of flowers, that stretched from one end of the valley to the other, gently bowing to the breeze that filled the valley. The inscription on the tablet called these flowers "peace be still."

There were all kinds of trees in this valley, and most of them looked like fruit trees. On these trees were all types of different fruit. There were hundreds of small trees in the valley. These trees were called "trees of joy." There were also hundreds of large trees, called "trees of love." There were bushes that stretched themselves along the streams of water, these bushes were called "security." In the middle of this beautiful valley was the oldest tree in the valley, and its branches reached to the heavens, this tree was called " long suffering."

Over on the east hill were different colored trees, the green trees were called "kindness," and the light blue trees were called "goodness"; to the west were trees called "faithfulness," "gentleness," and also "self-control." All of these trees were full of fruit, and you could eat to your heart's desire.

As I walked down into the valley, I could hear the sound of rushing water. The sound came from a stream, surrounded by the bushes called "security". This stream branched off and flowed through, and fed all the trees in the valley. These streams were no ordinary streams. They almost looked alive as they darted in and out of the trees. They were powerful streams, but gentle enough to walk across. They seemed to protect each tree, and give them strength. I walked up to one of the streams to take a drink. The water was cool and refreshing, and I could feel it flowing through my whole body. A sign near the edge of the water said, "O taste and see that the Lord is Good."

Enjoying every minute of this, I sat down amongst the flowers and the trees that seemed to have me hypnotized. I took out my Bible and read for a while and thought about how good God has been to me.

Next the rays of the sun filled the whole valley, and the sunshine consumed my whole body. For some reason this warm sensation made me feel very special, and that everything in this valley had been put here just for me. At that moment my relationship with God grew by leaps and bounds. I knew deep down in my heart that God had been with me all my life, even when I did not acknowledge Him. As tears of joy began to run down my face, a light rain began to fall. It felt like a cleansing, refreshing spray, which caused me to close my eyes and thank God for bringing me here to this wonderful point in my life.

As I stood there soaking up the sun's rays, feeling the light mist fall upon my face, and I watched the trees and the beautiful flowers paint a priceless picture in this valley. I knew for some reason, deep down in my soul, that everything was going to be all right.

After taking another drink of water, I lay down in the flowers called "peace be still." I closed my eyes and dozed off, falling into a deep sleep, I began to dream about where I had come from, and all that I had been through. Slowly it was revealed to me that God allowed me to go through all that I went through for a reason. This dream showed me that during the good times and the bad, God was with me all the time. In my sleep I was strengthened with peace, and joy! I dreamed about a better life serving God! I welcomed Him into my life, and on that day, I was filled with His precious Spirit! I awoke and began to praise God for my life. I praised Him for giving me another chance to get life right! For hours I praised His Holy Name. I even thanked God for getting high, smoking and drinking that the pain of that lifestyle ran me right into His arms.

I stayed on this floor, reading the Word of God, and tasting fruit from each tree for at least 3 months, before I decided it was time to move to the next floor.

As I walked out of this room, I noticed that I felt higher than I had ever felt in my entire life. I really didn't want to leave this room, but the process of recovery was far from being over. To be completely restored, I had to continue on to the other floors.

After leaving this very beautiful room, I headed back to the area where the elevators were stationed. Once in this hallway I noticed arrows pointing to another set of elevators. There was something different about these elevators.
1. The arrows on the outside of the elevator door now indicated "up" and "down."
2. As the doors opened, I saw these elevators were made of glass.

After getting on one of these glass elevators, the doors close slowly behind me. I pushed the button that said 4th floor. As it slowly started inching upward, I turned around and to my surprise I could see through this glass elevator, hundreds of other elevators, with passengers riding inside, some going up and some going down! The elevators that were going up, were taking passengers to different floors in this huge open space. I had to keep reminding myself that I was in a building. On some of the elevators, I could see the doors opening and the people getting off on different floors. As I looked through the top of this glass elevator, I could see some elevators going so high that they were going through the clouds!

Then there were the elevators that were going down. Inside these elevators, the passengers looked tired and confused, some looked weary, and some looked scared. These elevators did not stop; they went right to the basement. A label on top of the elevators going down read "STARTING OVER"!

Reality hit me like a ton of bricks "everybody was not making it." As I arrived at the 4th floor, butterflies feel my stomach, and I was hesitant in getting off.

The doors opened, and a young lady in a white suite who said, "Welcome to the Waiting room", greeted me. Then I was handed a card that I was told to keep with me always. That card read "The process of recovery is an ongoing process, Trust in God and continue!"

After receiving the card, I was led to another large room, where all types of activities were taking place. There were pool tables, game boards, big screen TVs and Ping-Pong tables. There were swimming pools, and people riding bikes. There was a weight lifting room where people were exercising. There where reading rooms, music rooms and computer rooms. People were buzzing around as if they did not have a care in the world! If I wished to access or participate in any of these activities, all I had to do was present the card that I received when I arrived on this floor to the attendant who worked in that particular area. The attendant in that area will ask you to present your card and read what is on your card! (The process of recovery is an ongoing process. Trust in God and continue) After you have done this, you may participate in any activity.

As I talked to some of the people here, I found out that some of them had been here for weeks, months, and even years! Some were not even thinking about leaving. After I made an attempt to visit every room, the fun began to wear off. Something was missing. In every room there were signs on the wall that read EASY DOES IT, BUT DO IT -- IT'S NOT OVER UNTIL IT'S OVER! -- DO YOU WANT TO GO HIGHER. KEEP PRESSING TOWARDS THE MARK!

I started thinking about some of the things I had learned on the other floors. Things like faith, stepping out into nothing to get to something.

Every time I wanted to participate in anything on this floor I had to read this card. Slowly it began to haunt my spirit.

(The process of recovery is an ongoing process. Trust in God and continue.) Every time I read this it reminded me that I still had work to do.

After reading these signs posted on every wall, and repeating what was on this card, I decided to step out on faith. I made my way to the elevator lobby. On the wall of the lobby there were even more signs. One said, "if you wish to continue, and have not applied the tools that you learned on the first 3 floors, you have three (3) options.

1. Continue on and GOOD LUCK!
2. Take the elevator to your right and push "arrow down" and start the process of recovery over from the first floor!
3. If you feel that you understand these steps and you are applying them in your life, you are ready to continue. Please take the elevators to the left, and push the button (arrow up!)

There was a sign on the outside of this elevator that read, "God will never leave you or forsake you!"

On the wall opposite the elevator, people gathered around to read the inscription. As they finished, some went back to the game room. Some sat and talked with each other. Some decided to start all over. As I approached this wall, the first thing I notice was bold letters that read:

THE FIRST THREE FLOORS INTRODUCE YOU
TO JESUS CHRIST OUR LORD AND SAVIOR!

THE NEXT FOUR FLOORS
WILL INTRODUCE YOU, TO YOU!

Ronald Simmons

And then it read:

About the 4th Floor.

1. You will take a trip back into your past. (Fear Not, God Is With You.)
2. You must be honest.
3. You must be thorough.
4. You must take notes.

Then it reads: Make sure you understand and remember these things:

1. God --

    (A) Personal Relationship With Him.
    (B) Know How To Contact Him.
    (C) Trust In him Always

2. Faith --

    (A) Always Believe Everything Is Going to Be All-Right.
    (B) Believing God Didn't Bring You This Far To Let You Go!

3. Power --

    (A) Defeated Death.
    (B) Protects The Saints.
    (C) Guides Your Path.

   While waiting for the elevator, I traded my game card for a "buzzer." This buzzer gave me direct access to someone who was just like me, but had already been through the Process of

Recovery. This person is called a "Sponsor." I could call on this person at anytime day or night!

Ronald Simmons

Fourth Floor

REVEALING WHO WE REALLY ARE!

As the elevator was taking me up, I boldly stood there waiting for the elevator doors to open! Once they opened, I was directed to an escalator. There was something strange about this escalator; I could only see 8 or 9 feet ahead of me. There was a desk and a chair stationed for me on the escalator. On the desk was a button, with the word "PRINT" beneath it. Also on the desk was a box of tissue. After taking my seat, I noticed a button near the arm of the chair that said "STOP" and "START." I was told at any time I could stop and examine my past.

Once I hit the "start" button, the escalator began to move, not very fast but at a nice and easy pace. The escalator went around a bend, and to my surprise a real live re-enactment of my life was beginning to take place. Every one in this play looked so real. There I was, a young kid growing up on the East Side of town. We were poor, but I did not know it. In this play my whole family was there. My mother and father, my brother and two sisters, were all there. My aunts and uncles, and cousins, and friends were there also. Even my dogs were there. Everyone looked so real. I yelled out to my Mom, but she could not hear me. I even whistled to my dogs but they could not hear me. The escalator began to slow up as it came upon the high and low points of my child hood. It showed my adolescent days, playing sports in the park, going fishing with my family, and playing house with my sisters (don't tell anyone I played house). It showed me shooting baskets in the backyard, dressing up in my father's clothes, hanging out with my friends on the block. It was all there, from the love of two parents giving me all the things I needed, and some of the things I wanted. Everything was not smooth in my past. Whether it was the pain of losing my best friend in an accidental shooting at the young age of 11 years old, or being teased for being too tall or too black, seems like it was always something: from the pain and frustration of watching two parents arguing, separating, and finally divorce. Memories of being molested, memories of being shot, or doing the shooting. Memories of spending time locked up in a jail cell alone and afraid far away from my family. The pain of all these memories began to overwhelm me.

The escalator begins to slow, and a slot on the desk that read "sponsor" card begin to flash. At this time I had an option to stop and talk to someone if I wished to, or continue on. I elected to continue on. I really just wanted to get through this!

As the escalator moved on, the memories of baseball games, and recital, with no one there to see me hit that home run, or sing that perfect note, began to play out before me, and the emptiness inside finally hit me as if it was yesterday!

The good and bad times were both there. Going through the day to day pain of a divorce, watching my family being torn apart, was not easy. These things continued to play out before me. I began to wonder why they kept repeating some of these scenes. Events that I did not want to deal with, kept coming back up. There were times when I had been hurt by mean people saying things like, "Your daddy wasn't nothing and you're not gonna be nothing." There were other things said like "Can't you do anything right" or "If I never would have had you, I wouldn't be in this problem I'm in!"

That was it, I could not take it any more, I needed to talk to someone, so I picked up my "Sponsor" card and put it in the slot. The escalator came to a halt, and my sponsor appeared and escorted me through an open door. Somehow we were back on the third floor. We sat down amongst the lilies, and the flowers, near a gentle stream. He reminded me that I was not alone, that the God that I had met on the third floor was with me. He reminded me of some of the dangerous situations that I had gotten myself into. It was only Jesus who delivered me.

Ronald Simmons

(Even when I didn't know Him) He then reminded me of some of the things that I had been introduced to on the first floor. Like acceptance--this is your past and it can't hurt you anymore. He told me that one good thing about the past; was that it had passed! Don't let it haunt you anymore!

He also reminded me of what I had learned on the second floor about "Faith." Every time I took a step, the light of courage came on! Then he reminded me about some of the things I had learned on this floor, the third floor. I looked around at the beautiful trees that I had fallen in love with, and the fruit that had been so refreshing to my soul! My sponsor made me realize that my pass could not hurt me, and I had to let the past go.

At this time, a plate was brought to me on a beautiful gold-leaf platter. On this platter, nestled in the flowers called "security," was some familiar fruit that I first saw and tasted on this third floor. There were a few slices of joy, a few slices of love and a few slices of faithfulness. A large glass of water was also given to me. This water was from the stream that protected the trees and the fruit. This water conquered fear, and gave strength, to that beautiful valley on the third floor. Of course I wanted to stay here on the third floor, but I knew that I must continue.

My sponsor then led me to this room called "Sharing." As I looked around the room I noticed some familiar faces. It was good to see that some of my friends who had started with me were still here. I also noticed that some of them were not there. Later on I found out that they had to start this process again. I wasn't mad at them, I knew that this was no easy task. So many times I wanted to quit and turn around.

As the meeting began, just like always, someone came out and began to share with us about her 4th floor experience. First she shared some demoralizing things that shocked me. I remember saying to myself, it takes a lot of courage to be that open and honest! But she did it with ease, and had a very sweet spirit. We could tell that none of these things that she was sharing were holding her captive anymore. Then she began to praise God for His goodness, and His grace. We all began to praise God for her freedom. It was at this point I discovered I wanted what she had. When she finished, no one felt less of her because of what she had shared. After she finished a man next to me stood up and talked about, how he had been covering up things in his past, until they began to over heat like a pressure cooker, and he became ill. This also caused him to become very angry, so he escaped by drinking and using. It sounds like he was telling my story. I now knew why they kept going back over some of the things in my past. I never wanted to face them, I just wished they would go away! So I stuffed them.

It was at this time, that I not only appreciated my relationship with God, but I needed God to help me make it through. I turned to my sponsor and asked him "Is it possible to go through recovery without God? And he said to me, "Yes you can, but those who make it live a bitter and angry life!" Always leaning to their own understanding."

On my way back to the fourth floor, I now understood why it was suggested that I take my time on the first through the third floors. It was important that I understood all the tools I had received. Without these tools, it seemed impossible to make it. Without these tools I would have surely turned back.

As I continued back into my past, some things were hard to deal with: broken hearts, fatherless or motherless times, molestation, destroyed dreams, mean people, and wrong discussions; depression, oppression, death of loved ones, wasted time and wasted years: bad memories of aborted babies' faces that haunted me in the night: behavior problems such as sexual misconduct, drug addiction, alcoholism, lying, cheating, stealing just to name a few. Now that these things had been revealed, I understood why I had done some of the things that I did, and had acted the way I acted. It was a miracle that I was still alive.

As the escalator came to a halt, finally, I was truly exhausted, numb, and guilty because of the way I had lived. My sponsor joined me at the escalator, and it took us to a large door that opened as we got closer. As I slumped down over this desk, it felt great to end this roller-coaster ride through my life. Thinking that this nightmare was all over, I saw the "PRINT" button on the desk light up and start flashing off and on. My sponsor hit the "Print" button and papers started coming out the side of the desk into a basket. It was a printed version of my whole life on paper! My sponsor gathered all the pages of my life, turned and walked off the escalator.

Suddenly it seemed as if I were having an anxiety attack! My heart seemed to be moving at a million miles a minute! This was getting to be too much! First, witnessing my whole life on screen, bringing back things that I had purposefully hidden in the back of my mind; now, this stranger picks up my whole life and walks off. This is too much!

My sponsor walked up to the elevators that went to the 5th floor. The doors immediately opened, and I followed him onto the elevator. My heart was still racing. My eyes were fixed on those several sheets of paper that seemed like everything to me!

Ronald Simmons

Fifth Floor

EXPOSING YOURSELF!

The doors opened onto the 5th floor. I followed my sponsor to a small boat; He stepped down into the boat and took a seat. I followed him right into the boat. There was no way I as letting him get away from me! I said nothing - he said nothing. I never took my eyes off my life tucked under his arms.

I never noticed that we were sitting on a large peaceful lake. I never noticed the mountains that surrounded this lake, and the many waterfalls that were coming off the mountain into the lake. I never saw the birds that were flying overhead or the clouds reaching to the heavens. All I could see was my life tucked under my sponsor's arms.

I never noticed that our boat had moved out into the lake and was slowly making its way out to the middle of the lake. My sponsor leaned over and handed me my life that was on paper. A sense of calm came over me, and I held on to those pages as if my life depended on it!

It was at this time I noticed my sponsor enjoying the beauty that surrounded us. The waterfall, the trees, the birds, how gentle and calm the water was. As I looked around on this large lake, there were other boats on the water. In each boat there were two people, floating around, not really going anywhere, but guided by some force going somewhere! On the side of each boat were the words "Let Go And Let God."

After a while my sponsor began to share with me. He started telling me things about his new life and where he had come from. As I sat there and listened again I wondered how he could freely share with me all of these demoralizing things that had taken place in his life. As I continued to listen to him, I recognized that the pain he went through was similar to mine. But his story was different.

He then shared with me that freedom and peace were just around the bend. And if I wanted this freedom and peace, all I had to do was surrender all those things, situations, hurts, and pain that had been holding me down. He told me to give them to God. God has been waiting for me to surrender these things to Him for years!

I replied that "this was easier said than done. These things have been with me most of my life." Then he replied, "it takes courage to let go of all your insecurities, pains, and fears. These deep-rooted emotions have been with you for most of your life. They made you who you are today."

Once I realized I had nothing to lose, (but self-destruction) I began to read my life history, to my sponsor. As the boat drifted aimlessly around the lake, fears tried to consume me, but I kept pressing on, sharing things that I had told myself I would never tell anyone!

As I got to the end of my life story, I buried my head in my paper. For some reason I felt dirty, and was embarrassed about my life. I also thought my sponsor was going to think less of me, or judge me, or even condemn me, because of what he had heard!

Slowly the boat started heading toward one of the waterfalls. The water falling off this particular fall was about 12 feet high, and looked like a long continual mirror falling gracefully into the lake. The sound of the waterfall splashing into the lake and the wind rushing through the trees seemed to hypnotize me as we got closer to the fall.

As we got closer to the waterfall my sponsor said nothing so I said nothing. Slowly the boat inched its way into the waterfalls. The water felt so good as it fell across by body. It was like being cleaned from head to toe, and I felt like a new person.

After going under the waterfall, we entered a cave that led to an opening back to the other side of the lake. The boat slowly drifted to the edge of a cliff where the water was falling into a big beautiful sea. Closer and closer we traveled towards this waterfall. My sponsor told me not to worry as the boat got closer. In a calm voice he said "how can a person have faith in God and worry at the same time." For some reason this made a lot of since to me. The boat began to stop right at the edge of the fall. The drop looked as if it were 7, or 8 stories down. The sound of the water crashing down below, and the white mist created by the fall, was electrifying.

My sponsor took my printed life story and began to rip the document into very small pieces. He then took the ripped pieces of paper, gave them to me, and told me to give them to God. At this time I threw them into the water. The force of the water took each piece around the boat and over the falls, which disappeared into the sea below. He then told me that I should never let my past hinder, or haunt me again! As I watched each piece fall into the sea below, a sense of closure fell upon me. I saw a sign on the bank of the shore that read "The Sea of Forgetfulness."

Slowly the boat turned around and headed back to the other side of the lake. A sense of peace came upon me, and a weight seemed as it were lifted off my shoulders.

I close my eyes and began to thank God for His goodness and for this knew life. For the first time in my life, I believed deep down in my soul that I was free. Once out of the boat, I was taken to an area that looked like the second and third floor combined. Here I was able to read and study, and live what I had learned and experienced so far in this process. Along with others, I was allowed to stay in these rooms for almost three months.

During this time I was encouraged to live my normal life. Everyday I worked, played, studied Gods Word, and spent time in the "sharing" room. For these three months my job was to live what I had learned. I was able to go to the "sharing" room as many times as I wanted. I could see that these sharing rooms were going to be a big part of my life, for the rest of my life. In the "sharing" room I slowly began to open up and talk about my past. In these rooms I felt comfortable, and safe. No one was looking down on me because we were all the same, and we had so much in common. We were all "hurting" people trying to get better.

When I felt it was time to move on to the next floor, I took my card and summoned my sponsor. He then led me to the elevators that went to the 6th floor. In my mind, I thought the rest of this process should be a breeze after what I went through on the 4th and 5th floors.

Once on the elevator my sponsor began to explain the process of recovery, and how it was a lifetime commitment. He praised me for allowing God to work in my life and change my life. He also told me that this journey was far from over. He told me that God was not finished revealing Himself to me and in these next two floors God was going to show me my own self!

While riding in this glass elevator, I could see that there were fewer elevators going to the top, and a lot more going back down starting over. Then he shared with me that even though God threw all past sins, hurt's, and fears into the "sea of forgetfulness," and there are some deep scars that still exist. These scars cause character defects that we do not realize we have. First these defects of character have to be recognized, and labeled. After you can call them by name, you have to make a decision on how you are going to eliminate them from your life. That is, if you really want to eliminate them from your life!

Ronald Simmons

Sixth Floor

REVEALING WHO YOU REALLY ARE!

Once the doors opened I stepped off into a hallway that led me to a large room. This room was set up like my old neighborhood. In this room I was allowed to work at my old job, and go to the same school I was going to before I dropped out because of my addiction. This allowed me to interact with my friends, and also my family. On this floor I was allowed to do everything I would do on a regular day to day basis. There was one thing that was different about this simulated life. Every time one of my character defects showed up, a mirror would show up. This mirror would flash before my eyes so that I could see the real me!

Each time the real me showed up a mirror would reflect my defect of character! I was well aware of some of these defects of character, and some of them I had no idea I had. Some of these defects of character were born from past pains in my life, and have been with me for a very long time. These mirrors would also explain why we act the way we act or how some of these defects of characters came about.

One mirror represented "defense." Every time someone got close to me I would push them away, one way or another! Some mirrors even revealed the reason. My "defense" mirror came up because of some mean things that had happened to me in my past because of mean people. Sometime unreliable people hurt me. People who said they were going to do one thing but did another. So this mirror called "defense" would appear every time someone would try to get close to me.

Subconsciously, I would push people away or sabotage a workable relationship.

Once again the "sharing" rooms were a big help to me. I was able to run to these rooms and discuss, and hear about other defects of character that I knew nothing about. Some mirrors were bigger than others, representing how great this character defect was part of my life and personality.

There was a medium size mirror that represented "arrogance" in my life. There was a large "prideful" mirror, and a large "selfish" mirror. These things were hard to swallow. There was a very large "lustful" mirror, and this mirror revealed why I treated the opposite sex the way I did. It was a wonder that I was even in a relationship.

Sometimes a small "lying" mirror would show up, or a medium "disobedient" mirror would appear. There was even a "lazy" mirror, and a "sensitive" mirror. People always told me that I was very sensitive, but I did not want to believe them.

Some days were better than others, but some days I could not take a step without a mirror appearing! After awhile I began to wonder if this correction would ever end! Day in and day out I was confronted with the real me.

Finally my sponsor showed up. He took me to another room where I was able to share with him about these defects of character that continued to appear. Was I really that bad? He told me that we were just in the beginning stages of this building process in my life. God was going to tear down some of the old building before he started building the new building, but He needed to make sure that I knew what they were before he started His work. After a very long talk he took me to the elevators that took me to the 7th floor.

Ronald Simmons

Seventh Floor

ELIMINATE THOSE THINGS THAT KEEP US FROM GROWING!

After getting on the elevator and arriving on the 7th floor, I noticed that the 6th and the 7th floor were just alike. Everything was the same; nothing had changed. After I had started my day to day routine one of my character defects showed up again. And later on, another defect showed up. Nothing had changed. I still had my character defects, and mirrors were showing up everywhere. Now there was even a new mirror, "Frustration."

Finally my sponsor showed up. In his hand was a small box that resembled a remote control. There was a button on top of this box, and when pushed a beam of light came out for about 20 feet. He began to walk through this life like seventh floor with me, and as he started to interact with other people, a mirror appeared. He paused for a minute and prayed, then he took the remote, pointed it towards the mirror and the light destroyed the mirror. He then turned and gave me the remote.

How could I be so arrogant, thinking that I could fix myself? Looking to God should always be the first thing I should do. Leaving out prayer is like, going into battle without a weapon! Frustrated I wondered if I were ever going to grasp this whole concept about the process, or about my walk with God.

Instead of going back to the 7th floor I went to what was becoming my new home, the "sharing" room. This time I stood up and talked about my fears, my fears of not making it, and returning to my old lifestyle. This time my answer came from an individual who was sitting in the audience. She talked about living "one day at a time." And how God wanted us to do our best, today! She went on talking about how living one day at a time made life easier for her. How just for today she did not have to participate in her disease. How just for today she was working on her character defects. She ended her speech with "yesterday is gone -- and tomorrow is not here -- live the best you can today!" Another person stood up and said, "the 6th floor was there for me to recognize my faults, or character defects." Here at the 7th floor he learned how to separate himself from them, and find a better way to deal with them.

After leaving the sharing room I ran back to the 7th floor to confront my issues. Unfortunately it did not take long for a mirror to appear. As I recognized what part I had to play in this situation I drop my head in prayer. I asked God to not only reveal my character defects, but also my motives behind why I was doing what I was doing. After praying, I raised my head and demolished the mirror with the remote. Every time one of my character defects appeared, I prayed and asked God to forgive me for my thoughts or my deeds. Then I "zap" destroyed the mirror. As the days went on I noticed there were fewer mirrors, because I was aware of the defect of character before it manifested itself. I also noticed how much prayer played a huge part in dealing with my defects of character. Now that my relationship with God had become a personal relationship, I wanted so much to please Him by changing or saying no to those things I knew were wrong! Every time I went before God about a defect, it made me work that much harder not to repeat it. Slowly, but surely, my life began to change.

In the beginning I got a kick out of blasting these mirrors into tiny pieces, but the ultimate joy was dealing with difficult situations, in a Godly manner. Being aware of these defects before I practiced them in my life was the greater reward. Also believing that one day God would say to me "Well-done thy good and faithful servant."

I could not wait to get back to my "sharing" room, and to my surprise, they asked me to share about the good things that I had been introduced to on the 7th floor. I share about praying first when someone brought out the anger in me, and how I did not re-act, and to my surprise the mirror did not appear. I shared how I had to give, so that "selfish" mirror wouldn't appear. I shared how I was still in the process of understanding humility so that the "pride" mirror wouldn't show up as much. And when beautiful women, cross my path it was OK to recognize that they looked good, but I had to learn how to leave it right there, and move on! This was going to take a whole lot of practice! I mean a whole lot of practice.

After I finished sharing, my sponsor walked up to me and told me that I was on the right track! He also told me that it is almost impossible to perfect this part of the process, but our goal is to continue to strive for perfection. On the 7th floor, you must show signs of progress before you move on to the next floor, and it was time for me to move on.

As I stepped on to this glass elevator, most of the elevators going up were unlike the elevators on the earlier floors. Looking up through the top of the elevator, I could see sunlight filling the sky. The suns' rays engulfing each elevator that inched its way up through the clouds. Once again I felt as if I were going in the right direction.

Ronald Simmons

Eighth Floor

WHAT PART DID YOU HAVE TO PLAY IN IT?

As the elevator came to a halt, a sign inside it read "Where There Is Smoke, There Is Fire." I had been in this process now for almost a year, and I knew that something weird was about to happen. This time my spirit was ready. God had brought me a long way, and it was time for me to trust Him. I bowed my head and prayed that God would continue to guide me and teach me, and I thanked Him in advance for what was about to happen! "So bring it on!" Before I could get the words out of my mouth, the doors opened. The smell of smoke was thick in the air. This elevator let me out on a small hill that overlooked a valley. Down in the valley, there was a lake and around that lake were small fires burning out of control. The sky was filled with black smoke. As I looked to the right of me, I could see another elevator sitting far off on top of another hill. This person, like my self was standing at the entrance of the elevator looking down into another valley, where smoke was filling the sky. I wish I could tell you that I was ready to run down into the valley and see what was going on, but instead, there was some fear growing inside. I bowed my head and prayed to the Father, and asked Him to guide and protect me as I continued on in this world called recovery.

After praying I took the trail that led me down to what looked like my own private lake. The closer I got to the lake the thicker the smoke became. The lake was about as big as a football field. The fire was coming from many bridges that connected one side to the other. On the other side of the lake, a person stood at the end of each bridge, and each bridge was on fire. The smoke was too thick to make out who these people were. Some of these bridges were completely demolished, some were halfway destroyed, and some looked like they had not been burning very long. As I stood there, not knowing what to do, my sponsor walked up to me, (Thank God) and began to explain to me what was taking place. He told me that each person standing across the lake was someone special in my life that I had harmed. They were people who trusted in me, that I either, lied to, stolen from, or hurt in some way or another. And because of my using, and the way I was living I had almost destroyed my relationship with them. He led me to the edge of the first bridge, at the edge of the water. There was a desk, a chair, and paper and pencil, and also a slot right in the middle of the desk. Also on the desk was the name of the person standing across from me. In this case it was my father. As I looked across the lake I could barely see him because of the smoke. The bridge in this case was 60% gone, and a small fire was still burning on the bridge. I looked up at my sponsor with tears in my eyes, as I started to think about the things that I had done to my father, and what an embarrassment I had become. I picked up my pencil and began writing. I started off by writing down how I thought he did not spend enough time with me, and how it hurt me that he missed my football games etc. My sponsor looked down at the paper. He then took the paper from me and destroyed it. He told me that this was not about what I thought my father did to me, but about what I did to him as a son. He reminded me that we went through all of that on the 4th floor!   Today we seek forgiveness. Humility comes when we are able to see what part we had to play in the break down of a relationship. Did I disrespect him or his house? Or did I lie to him? Did I steal from him? He then explained that this part of the recovery process is a healing process, but it's also a growing process, for me. We have to learn how to forgive ourselves, and stop beating ourselves up for what we did in the past. At the same time we have to accept the fact that some bridges may never be put back together. For some of our loved ones, and friends, the pain is too great, and they would rather not be bothered with us ever again. But the attempt at reconciliation still has to be made. As long as we know that we have done all we could do in mending this relationship, we can go on with life, feeling better about ourselves.

After that speech my sponsor disappeared again. I then turned towards my father and took the pencil in hand and began to write.

This time I started off by asking my father (on paper) to forgive me for all the things that I had done. In some cases I even figured out how to make restitution for some of the things I had taken. As I began to write, some deep-rooted confrontations started spilling out on this paper. I began to see just what part I had to play in each confrontation.

Once I had finished my sponsor appeared again. He took the few pieces of paper and dropped them in the slot in the desk. We then walked over to the next bridge. My mother's name was on this desk. After going through my whole family, and friends I was mentally drained and felt so small that I could play handball against the curb.

My sponsor appeared and took me to the "sharing" room. I sat down in the back of the room, not feeling very good about myself. People were sharing about their 1st floor experiences, 5th floor experiences, and so on. I listened to people share about leaving this building called recovery because they thought they were ready to face the world. I listened to people who were in this building called recovery for the 2nd and 3rd time.

At that time, I began to pray that God would forgive me for being such a jerk, and I asked Him to help me make it through this hard time, that I was experiencing. I also prayed for some of the people who were in this sharing room. Those who were thinking about leaving recovery, and also those who were struggling, doing there best to get it right this time. Finally the main speaker came out and shared his experience, strength and hope with the group. In his testimony he shared that he had lost his immediate family at a very early age. That was enough for me to hear. Here I was feeling sorry for myself, about some of the things that I had done to my loved ones, and how hard it was going to be to apologize to them. This person wished he had some loved ones to apologize to. That was enough for me to be grateful. After I had been in that room for a while my sponsor appeared. He shared with me, that by writing down the wrongs that I had done to my loved ones, I had completed the 8th floor. He told me that I had to recognize my wrongs before reconciliation could take place.

It was now time to move on to the 9th floor. My sponsor shared with me that, at the 9th floor, it was time for me to humble myself and personally ask my family members, my loved ones, and friends for forgiveness. After we prayed, the doors of the elevator opened on to the 9th floor.

Ronald Simmons

Ninth Floor

I APOLOGIZE!

To my surprise, I had returned to the 8th floor, or what looked like the 8th floor. The lake, the cloudy skies, the bridges on fire, they were all there. But this time I was on the other side of the lake. There in front of me was my father sitting at a desk, in front of the burning bridge. As I got closer to him, I could see that he was reading the paper that I had written to him and dropped into the slot. Before I could turn and run, he looked up and saw me standing there. He stood up and started walking towards me. My legs were frozen and I could not move. Before I could apologize, he put his arms around me and told me all was forgiven. He began to apologize for things that he had done and said in the past. At this time, unknown to me, the fire on the bridge was out and the bridge was slowly putting itself back together. We talked for a long time and promised each other to spend more time together.

The same thing happened with most of my friends and loved ones. All they wanted from me, was a committed, and honest, lifestyle. In most cases, the fires went out and the bridges were coming together slowly. Some more slowly than others, but this was understood. I knew in some cases, that it was going to take some time. Some had heard my apologies before, so there was very little trust. Then there were others, who weren't so thrilled about this recovery process that I was going through. But I was sure that if I continued to be all that God would have me to be, they would also see the change. I would never forget this day, the day God gave me my family back!

At this time I was led down another hallway. At the end of that hallway were two doors; one said "sharing" room, the other said "2nd floor." This time I decided to go to the second floor where I was able to study God's Word. I was eager to investigate Gods Love through forgiveness, and understand why He loved people who were so rebellious. I stayed here for a few days, enjoying God's Word, and with every sentence I was built up, with hope, and was encouraged to go higher in my recovery.

After walking out of that room, I ended up right where I left off, in the hallway on the 9th floor. I walked over to the elevators, but changed my mind and went into the "sharing" room. There I saw some familiar faces. We were able to talk about this new life in Christ, and this process we were going through called recovery. The meeting began, and to my surprise the main speaker of this meeting was my sponsor. He briefly talked about how he got here, the pain, the hard times, and his life as an alcoholic/addict. He also talked about his relationship with God, and how living the Word was one of the most important things that a Christian in recovery could do. He talked about the difference in applying the Word of God in your life, rather than just reading It, and memorizing the Word of God. You could hear a pin drop, as he talked about how important "change" is to a recovering person. He finished by saying, "to walk out of this building and not change according to the Word, would be a waste of time for all of us! And all your pain and suffering, that you came into this building with, would gladly be refunded to you if you did not change!"

Once he finished speaking, we all went to our individual glass elevators. Once on, the doors closed slowly behind me. It took me up through the clouds. The sun was shining ever so brightly, and as far as the eye could see, there were elevators going up through the clouds. It was a great day to be alive and an even better day to be a Christian.

As the elevator began to stop, a sign appeared on a message board. It read welcome to the 10th floor, you have almost completed your journey, but it is not over yet.

Ronald Simmons

Tenth Floor

WILL THE REAL YOU PLEASE STAND UP!

Once the doors opened, my sponsor met me. I told him that I enjoyed what he had shared in the "sharing" room and I thanked him for spending all this time with me. Then he said something that I will never forget. He said in order to keep the peace that I have and the freedom that I have, I must give it away! He told me that our God was a giving God, and that our job is to be more like Him. Time, money, our lives were all given to us by God. We who were addicted to drugs or alcohol, lived close to death, had no hope, and God came into our lives and clearly rescued us, should work even harder in giving back to God.

As we walked down the hallway, we approached a large door. He then told me that he was going to accompany me on this floor. As the doors opened, we walked through this large door, and I could see several large glass-like bubbles. Each glass bubble enclosed a place that was very familiar to me!

One was my apartment that I had lived in years ago. The other looked like a construction site where I was once employed. The other was my current home. There were several more glass bubbles but from where we were standing I could not see what or who was in them.

As we approached this glass bubble that enclosed my apartment, my sponsor and I took a seat on a couch right outside this bubble. Before I could ask what was going on, my front door opened and to my surprise, I walked through that door, or someone who looked like me walked through that door. I looked to my sponsor and he said that it was me.

As the other "me" walked through the door, the first thing he, I, did was grab the remote control, flop down on the couch and turn on the TV. After flipping the channels and finally settling with the news, I got up and went into the kitchen, fixed a meal, and came back into the TV area. After eating, spending some time on the phone, and looking at a number of TV shows, the door bell rang, and it was a couple of very good friends, Derrick and Mark. We sat around looking at TV and drinking a couple of beers. Derrick pulled out a couple of joints, which we smoked. After a few hours of sitting around talking, both Derrick and Mark decided to leave. After they left, I got on the phone and asked a girl friend to come by. After she arrived, I persuaded her to spend the night with me. At this time the glass bubble went black.

    I looked to my sponsor and told him, "this was the old me, and now I have changed!" He asked me how I felt as I watched myself in action. He then asked me what part of this recreation I didn't like. Of course I did not like drinking beer, and smoking dope, and fornicating at the end.
He then told me "yes, these things were problems but there were some other things that need my attention."

1. My relationship with the TV: I had to consider the hours that I spent glued to this large box.
2. My relationship with my friends: How I had to separate myself from them, because of my new life in Christ.
3. How I used women to satisfy my own selfish needs.

He then told me that, honestly examining myself was going to play a big part in my growth as a Christian.
    We then moved to a couch right outside the next glass bubble. This bubble enclosed a job site that I had recently worked on, where we were building some condominiums in Malibu, California.
    After we took our seats I could see myself pulling up to the job site a few minutes late. As far as I could see, there weren't any big problems. I was one of the lead men on this

job, and I was very good at framing houses. I was well liked by my employer and the persons that I worked with. As this day began to unfold, my interaction with the men on the job was fairly normal. As I examined myself I noticed that there was one area that I needed to work on, and that was my language. At the end of the day, when we were off the clock, I spent some time laughing and talking with some of the workers on the site. Some of them were drinking, and using, but this was something that I did not do. Soon after this day was over, the glass bubble went black and this part of the process was over.

My sponsor then asked me to examine the day. I told him that because I was a Christian, cussing could not be part of my vocabulary anymore. Other than that I did not notice anything wrong. He told me that there were several things that he noticed in my life, and that he suggested I change.

1. Being late on the job. And my attitude towards the job. He then told me that God gave me the job, so I should work as if I reported to God Himself.
2. That I should stop trying to fit in with people who did not believe in living righteous, and Holy. He told me that it was OK to have friends in the world, but we should never conform to the world and always stand up for what is Godly right.

He also shared that the company I was working for paid me for eight hours, and I should give them eight hours.

He said that because I was a Christian, I had to carry myself like a Christian. Sometimes people were going to shun me, talk about me and say things about me that were not true, but all this came with the territory of being a Christian.

After he finished, a light came on in the glass bubble next to us. It was my home that I lived in now. As we approached the bubble, I could see myself, my wife, and my kids sitting around the dinner table. As we took our seats outside the bubble, I began to listen in on the conversation that was coming from that dinner table. I noticed how I was dictating the conversation at the table, and no one else had an opinion. I could see that I was a talker and not a listener. I noticed my son and daughter giving me yes and no answers, not really participating in the conversation.

I turned to my sponsor and asked him was I really that bad. The light went dim in my house, and my sponsor walked with me to the end of the room where there was a door that led to either the "sharing" room or the elevator. I chose the sharing room. This time I raised my hand to share. I talked about how hard it was going to be for me to change, but I had no other alternative. I wanted to become a better person.

After sharing, I listened to a couple of other speakers and I decided to move on to the next floor.

Eleventh Floor

WORK ON YOURSELF!

Once the doors opened onto the eleventh floor, I walked up to another large door. When these doors opened, I found myself standing in a large cathedral. Down in front of the altar there were people on their knees praying to God. I knew that for this transformation to take place in my life, an everyday communication with God was going to have to take place. There were so many bad habits that I had acquired over the years. I needed God to be with me, share with me, go with me, stay with me, correct me and guide me. I ran down to that altar and fell on my face and prayed to God. I stayed there for what seemed like hours. After praying, I got up and noticed my sponsor on his knees, praying next to me. I was reminded of a bumper sticker that read "a family that prays together stays together." I began to thank God for my sponsor being in my life. Spending valuable time with me, walking and talking and being there for me. I walked out of that cathedral with a renewed spirit.

From there I went to the (2nd) second floor, and studied God's Word. My sponsor suggested I do a word search on "Gods love." I spent hours and hours, and it seemed like days went by yet I had only scratched the surface. I was amazed by every chapter, every verse, and every psalm that I read--because God's love was in it.

After leaving the 2nd floor, I went into the "sharing" room. It was good to see a few familiar faces in the room. Some of these people had started when I started, and I could see the joy of the Lord on their faces. Today people were sharing about how good God was, and how much He loved us even when we did not deserve it.

Finally it was time to move on to the 12th floor. I met my sponsor at the elevator and he gave me a big hug, and told me that this was it, the last floor. We entered the elevator for the last time. As the doors closed, I began to think about the beginning of this journey, and where God had brought me. I also thought about all of the floors that I had been on. Tears began to run down my face as I thought about my new relationship with God, and how in working and living this process, God had renewed my life and my mind. I knew deep down in my heart that God really loved me! But for what reason I had no clue!

Ronald Simmons

Twelfth Floor

GET TO WORK!

After the door closed, my sponsor pushed the button to the 12th floor. Slowly it began to move. As we looked out over this beautiful building, my sponsor began to remind me that it was God that put this process of recovery together for addicts and alcoholics who had a hard time living! As I looked through the glass at Gods glory, I began to praise Him openly!

Still moving upwards he talked about how many people will never know God and experience His goodness and His power. He told me that it was my job to carry the message of freedom to the addict/alcoholic who was still suffering.

As we slowly inched our way up in the elevator, he talked about the enemy, satan, who was very upset with this new relationship I had with God, and how he was going to do everything in his power to steal this new joy from me. He told me that drugs and alcohol were not my problem any more. Satan usually attacks in the area of disobedience, and if I did not examine myself daily, and repent, drugs and alcohol usage is right around the corner!

He then told me to never forget my sharing rooms! He made it very clear to me that these rooms could save my life. I was far from being what God wanted me to be, and the only way to stay free is to be honest around people who understood me.

When the doors open onto the 12th floor, there was something very strange but familiar about this floor. A dark mist seemed to hover over the room, and the light was very dim.

As I looked, around I could see people with no joy, and no hope, on their faces. On the other side of the room there was an elevator. Above the elevator was an arrow pointing up.

I could see people standing at the doors waiting for the doors to open. Others were sitting in corners and lying on benches, and some were not even trying to get on to the elevator.

"Lord have mercy" I was back in the basement. Back in the very same place that I had started over a year ago.

A weird feeling came over me and I looked to my sponsor and he told me it was my turn to help someone. It was my turn to give back what had been so freely given to me.

He told me that in order to keep this peace and freedom that I had, I must give everything I learned in this building away!

He then told me to take my pick, and he pointed to the addicts/alcoholics in the basement. Then he turned around and got back onto the elevator and left me there to help someone, and start the rest of my life!

As the elevator doors began to close, he said, "If you ever wonder why your life was spared from a horrible death, or if you ever wonder what your calling is, remember this..." and the doors closed before he could finish!

But in large white letters on the now closed doors read "YOU WERE SAVED TO SERVE GODS PEOPLE."

I turned back around and noticed a guy sitting in a corner crying his eyes out. I also noticed another guy looking for food in a trash can.

A scripture came to mind "the harvest is surely ripe, but the labors are few!
TIME TO GET BUSY!

Chapter Sixteen

WHAT DID YOU LEARN FROM THIS PROCESS CALLED RECOVERY AND HOW CAN IT HELP YOU?

I hope you enjoyed this fictional walk through the process of recovery. I thank God for speaking to me in the way that he did.
Now we must take a look at some key points.

For the Addict/Alcoholic:

1. The process of recovery is an on going process, which is never ending.
2. You can not get this thing called "recovery" over night.
3. You must have a sponsor.
4. You must make meetings, and participate in these meeting, by getting honest and sharing.
5. Live the Word, and you will be free!
6. You must change!
7. It takes work!
8. Remember this disease of addiction is a sickness.

For the family member:

1. Allow the recovering person to make as many meetings as possible.
2. When they are not making meetings, they are in relapse mode.
3. Do not, (repeat) Do not work their program for them.
4. Do not, (repeat) Do not work their program with them. Don't go to their meetings with them; don't volunteer to be their sponsors.
5. Don't be afraid to ask, "what step are they on.
6. Get to know their sponsor. Ask the sponsor to be honest with you and call you if he stops making his meeting.
7. This process of recovery takes time.
8. Remember this disease of addiction is a sickness.

Church Auxiliary Leader:

If you know of a person who comes out of a recovery home you can request:

1. Recovery Card. This card will list the meetings this person is attending. We suggest 3 meeting a week, bible study and Church on Sunday. (See back page)
2. This is between you and the recovering person. No one else should know unless he decides to tell someone.
3. If you observe that he is not attending his meetings, have a talk with him as soon as possible.
4. Remember this disease of addiction is a sickness.

Employers:

If the recovering person comes back from a leave of absent, because of his addiction, or you find that he has a problem, please consider the following:

1. Recovery Card. This card will list the meetings this person is attending. (See back page)
2. This is between you and the recovering person. No one else should know unless he decides to tell someone.
3. Remember the disease of addiction.

RECOVERY CARD
(Church/Employers name and phone number)

     This card is used not to embarrass the recovering person that is using it. We hope that this will help them become apart of a process that can shape their lives. The Recovering person should turn this card in before every meeting. No facilitator should sign this card, if cardholder is over 15 minutes late for the meeting.

NAME OF MEETING	DATE	FACILITATORS SIGNATURE
1.		
2.		
3.		
4.		
5.		
6.		
7.		
8.		
9.		
10.		
11.		
12.		

Ronald Simmons

Comming April 1st 2000

There Is A Ram In The Bush
"The Workbook"

A working guide through the process of recovery and the 12 Spiritual Ways to freedom.

Call and order 310 764-4400 or e-mail at freenone@msn.com